WOMEN &
US POLITICS

SECOND EDITION

WOMEN &
US POLITICS

The Spectrum of
Political Leadership

Lori Cox Han

LYNNE
RIENNER
PUBLISHERS

BOULDER
LONDON

Published in the United States of America in 2010 by
Lynne Rienner Publishers, Inc.
1800 30th Street, Boulder, Colorado 80301
www.rienner.com

and in the United Kingdom by
Lynne Rienner Publishers, Inc.
3 Henrietta Street, Covent Garden, London WC2E 8LU

Library of Congress Cataloging-in-Publication Data
Han, Lori Cox.
 Women and US politics : the spectrum of political leadership / Lori Cox
Han. — 2nd ed.
     p. cm.
 Rev. ed. of : Women and American politics : Boston : McGraw-Hill, c2007.
 Includes bibliographical references and index.
 ISBN 978-1-58826-735-1 (pb : alk. paper)
 1. Women—Political activity—United States. 2. Political leadership—
United States. I. Han, Lori Cox, Women and American politics. II. Title.
 HQ1236.5.U6H34 2010
 320.973082—dc22

                                                          2009044603

British Cataloguing in Publication Data
A Cataloguing in Publication record for this book
is available from the British Library.

Printed and bound in the United States of America

            The paper used in this publication meets the requirements
  ∞   of the American National Standard for Permanence of
            Paper for Printed Library Materials Z39.48-1992.

     5   4   3   2   1

For my daughter,
Taylor Ann NyBlom

Contents

Tables

Preface

As I began the process of revising this text for its second edition, it was striking how many significant and historic changes had occurred for women in US politics since the final draft of the first edition was completed in the spring of 2005. At that point, scholars and political pundits alike could only imagine if and/or when Nancy Pelosi might become the first woman speaker of the House and whether or not Hillary Rodham Clinton might actually run for president in 2008. In addition, foreign policy and national security dominated the political agenda at the start of the second term of the George W. Bush presidency, and with a Republican-controlled Congress, much speculation focused on the possibility of a permanent conservative majority. Five years later, in the spring of 2010, the political landscape has changed dramatically thanks to the Democratic Party winning Congress in 2006 and the White House in 2008, which has brought with it a major shift in the policy agenda toward domestic and economic matters (a shift due also, in part, to the economic meltdown throughout 2008).

During that same time period, many more barriers were broken for women in the political arena, including Pelosi's ascent to speaker of the House in 2007 (making her the highest-ranking woman in the history of the federal government), Clinton's campaign for the Democratic nomination (during which she earned 18 million votes and won 21 primary contests), Sarah Palin's nomination for vice president (making her the first woman nominated for vice president by the Republican Party and the first woman nominated by a major party since Geraldine Ferraro in 1984), and

Sonia Sotomayor's confirmation as the first Latina to serve on the US Supreme Court. Several women took key positions in the new Obama administration, and women in both parties continue to make slow but steady progress in gaining access to political power through elected and appointed positions at all levels of government. While the historic nature of the achievements of high-profile women in the political process has tended to dominate the headlines during the last few years, it is perhaps the fact that Americans are becoming much more accustomed to seeing women in these top political positions that is the more compelling story. While much remains to be done in achieving political equity between the sexes, it is important to remember that just a few years ago, it would have been difficult to imagine such achievements. As such, women as political participants, and even more importantly as political leaders, continue to be an important topic of study for not only political scientists but even the most casual of political observers.

Political leadership has always been a prominent theme in my women and politics course, as well as in other courses that I teach and in my research as a presidency scholar. My interest in the topic of political leadership also drives my teaching and scholarly interests in terms of women and politics, particularly the intersection of the subfield with that of presidential studies when considering the question of electing the first woman president. Leadership in and of itself is a fascinating topic for political scientists as we seek to better understand the unique dynamics of the concept, exploring not only how such a malleable term should be defined, but what role, if any, it plays in shaping our governing institutions. This text is an attempt to capture that theme in a way that will help students to better understand the role that women have played and are currently playing in the US political process and if their presence has brought with it any significant changes in public policies or how our governing institutions operate. The areas and themes included in the book provide the essential broader topics for teaching a women and politics course, while also considering the issue of women's leadership as a core theme and mode of analysis as more women get elected to office (Congress and state governorships) and appointed to high-ranking federal positions (in the executive and judicial branches), and as the United States moves closer to electing the first woman president.

There are many areas of research in a variety of disciplines focusing on women, gender, and feminism, and many of them intersect with a discussion of women in US politics. My goal in writing this book is to provide an interesting, lively, and timely discussion of contemporary political issues in the United States that involve women as political participants, candidates, and officeholders, as well as to make the book readable and accessible to students at all levels. I hope to have provided just enough historical context to get students interested in the evolution of women in US political life, so that they will seek more information and knowledge on this important topic. The study of women and politics has emerged as a powerful voice within the discipline of political science in the past few decades, and I hope that readers find this text a useful addition to the ongoing dialogue and that instructors find it to be a useful pedagogical tool for their courses.

Many people deserve to be acknowledged for playing an important role in the development and evolution of this project. The editorial team at Lynne Rienner exemplifies professionalism in academic publishing, and from the start I knew that this second edition would be in excellent hands. I would like to thank Leanne Anderson in particular for her support and helpful suggestions for revising and updating the book. In addition, I still owe a debt of gratitude to Monica Eckman for helping to develop the text the first time around. I am also grateful to the many friends and colleagues with teaching and research interests in the subfield of women and politics for sharing their perspectives and suggestions, including Ann Gordon at Chapman University, Diane Heith at St. John's University, and Caroline Heldman at Occidental College. Their expertise on this topic has been invaluable, and I am truly blessed by their continued friendship and support. Finally, as always, I thank my husband, Tom, and my children, Taylor and Davis, for their never-ending love and support and for all the sacrifices made for this book and those that came before it.

WOMEN &
US POLITICS

1

Women and Political Leadership

The only safe ship in a storm is leadership.
■ Faye Wattleton, president of the
Center for the Advancement of Women

The 2008 presidential election made history on many levels. Barack Obama was elected the first African American president, Hillary Rodham Clinton became the first truly competitive woman candidate seeking the presidency, Sarah Palin became the first Republican woman to be nominated for vice president, and the campaign itself was both the longest and most expensive in US history. At the congressional level, the 2008 election outcome meant that more women than ever before would be serving in the US Congress. At the start of the Obama administration in January 2009, several women were appointed to prominent positions in the cabinet and as White House advisers, and when faced with his first Supreme Court vacancy a few months later, President Obama nominated Judge Sonia Sotomayor to become the third woman (and first Latina) to serve on the nation's highest court. Generally speaking, the 2008 elections represented a significant moment for women in US politics as they continued to earn positions of political power, even if their progress overall has been slower than many Americans would like. In addition, the historic campaigns of both Clinton and Palin focused tremendous attention on the topic of women as political leaders as voters assessed these two candidates with vastly different life experiences, governing styles, and ideological perspectives. While neither candidate won the office

1

that each sought, the significant roles that both played in the presidential campaign broke through barriers and showed the success
that women are now capable of having on the national political
stage.

In the aftermath of Clinton's presidential campaign—during
which she received 18 million votes in the Democratic primary
contest—Palin's rise as a political star in conservative Republican
circles, and Nancy Pelosi's historic ascent to speaker of the House
in 2007, political pundits and scholars alike have been intrigued
by the idea of women as political leaders and by the question of
what changes, if any, would occur in the political arena if women
held more positions of power. In recent years, several books and
articles have been devoted to the simple question, what if women
ran the world?[1] Similarly, if every position of political leadership
in the United States, whether elected or appointed, were suddenly
held by a woman—not only the president but all of the cabinet
and advisory positions, all of the leadership positions in Congress
(including speaker of the House and the Senate majority leader),
and all nine seats on the US Supreme Court, along with every
state governorship, every leadership position in each of the fifty
state legislatures, and every mayoral position in every city across
the country, would the US governing and political processes, as
well as the public policy agenda, suddenly change? And if so,
would it improve by becoming more efficient and effective?

While theoretically this kind of extreme shift in political leadership is possible, it is probably unlikely. Women in the United
States, who have only had the right to vote since 1920, are still
struggling to reach parity with, let alone dominance over, their
male counterparts in political leadership positions. In theory,
democratically elected political bodies should look something like
the larger society that they represent. This provides legitimacy to
political institutions, particularly in regard to women, who make
up slightly more than half of the US population. However, thinking about such an extreme shift in the political landscape is quite
instructive, since it was not that many years ago that men held
every political leadership position in Washington, DC. The
thought of every position of power being held by a woman raises
some interesting questions. Does gender matter when electing
political leaders? Perhaps more important, how do Americans
view women as political leaders, and how does this view impact

women's chances of success within the political arena? And finally, in a political age so driven by the influence of the news media, do negative stereotypes about women as political officeholders and power brokers harm women's career opportunities in the public sector? These questions are crucial when studying the role of women in US politics, since not only do women have the right as citizens to political participation but full participation by women as both voters and officeholders has an important impact on the political process and on the outcome of important public policy debates.

■ Women as Political Leaders: A Historical Perspective

According to political scientist Barbara Kellerman, while few women have held formal positions of authority throughout world history, that is "not tantamount to saying they did not exercise power or exert influence."[2] Similarly, progress has been made in the past half-century, but only when including both informal as well as formal positions of influence within government, business, nonprofits, and religious organizations, with more women at the bottom as opposed to the top of most organizational hierarchies.[3] The traditional view of US politics suggests that those with political power are those who hold specific leadership positions within government. From that vantage point, how have women fared?

Within the executive branch, no woman has ever been elected president or vice president, whereas only three women have ever served as secretary of state (Madeleine Albright, Condoleezza Rice, and Hillary Rodham Clinton) and one as attorney general (Janet Reno). These latter two cabinet positions, along with secretary of defense and secretary of the treasury, are considered the most prominent among the now fifteen cabinet-level departments in the executive branch. And the three most recent presidents (at the time of this writing) made these four appointments—with Albright and Reno serving in Bill Clinton's administration, Rice serving in George W. Bush's administration, and Clinton in Barack Obama's administration—which means that this has been a fairly new trend. The early cabinet appointments of Frances

Perkins by Franklin Roosevelt in 1933 (to secretary of labor) and Oveta Culp Hobby by Dwight Eisenhower in 1953 (to secretary of health, education, and welfare, which is now split between the Departments of Health and Human Services and Education) are considered political anomalies; the next woman to be appointed to a cabinet position would not come until 1975, when Gerald Ford selected Carla Anderson Hills as secretary of housing and urban development. In total, forty women have held forty-five cabinet or cabinet-level positions (including the positions of United Nations ambassador, national security adviser, special/US trade representative, director of the Office of Management and Budget, chair of the Council of Economic Advisors, administrator of the Environmental Protection Agency, administrator of the Small Business Administration, and director of the Office of Personnel Management) since 1933.

Special advisers within the White House are often considered even more powerful and influential than cabinet appointments. No woman has ever served as chief of staff; only two women have served as presidential press secretary (Dee Dee Myers served as Clinton's press secretary from 1993 to 1994, and Dana Perino served as George W. Bush's press secretary from 2007 to 2009); and only one has served as the national security adviser (Condoleezza Rice served in this role during George W. Bush's first term from 2001 to 2005). Karen Hughes, who held the joint title of director of communications and counselor to the president for George W. Bush from 2001 until her resignation in 2003, is considered one of the most influential women to ever serve in an advisory capacity to a president within the Oval Office. Similarly, Valerie Jarrett, who holds the position of senior adviser and assistant to the president for public engagement and intergovernmental affairs, is one of only three senior advisers to President Barack Obama.

In the judicial branch, only three women have ever served on the US Supreme Court: Sandra Day O'Connor, nominated by Ronald Reagan in 1981; Ruth Bader Ginsberg, nominated by Bill Clinton in 1993; and Sonia Sotomayor, nominated by Barack Obama in 2009. In the legislative branch, no woman had ever held a top leadership position until Nancy Pelosi's (D-California) ascent in 2003 to Democratic minority leader in the House of Representatives. Pelosi went on to become speaker of the House of Representatives in 2007, a position she holds at the time of this writing in 2009, and she remains the only woman ever to hold a congressional leadership post. At the state level, only thirty-one women have ever served as governors, and Ella Grasso's election as the Democratic governor of Connecticut in 1975 marked the first time that a woman was elected to the top state executive position in her own right, without replacing her husband in office (due either to his death or his inability to succeed himself).

Since the days of Nellie Tayloe Ross (D-Wyoming) and Miriam "Ma" Ferguson (D-Texas), both elected in 1925 as governors of their respective states to succeed their husbands, and of Frances Perkins, who made history as the first woman cabinet member in Washington, women have made tremendous progress, at least statistically, in gaining access to elective or appointed office at most levels of government. Yet reaching a level of parity that is representative of the population at large, in which women voters slightly outnumber male voters, is still many decades away. And due to recent gains for women in elected positions, public perceptions seem to indicate that most Americans believe that women are receiving equal treatment in regard to leadership opportunities in both the public and private sectors. According to the Center for American Women and Politics, as of July 2009, there are now more women serving in the US Congress than ever before—seventeen in the Senate and seventy-two in the House of Representatives. In addition, a total of seventy-three women hold statewide executive positions, 1,792 women serve as state legislators, and eleven women serve as mayors of the hundred largest US cities.

As impressive as those numbers may be, however, the percentages tell a different story. Of the 535 seats in the US Congress, women hold only 16.6 percent. Of statewide executive positions such as governor, lieutenant governor, and attorney general, only 23.6 percent are held by women (and only six of fifty governors are women). A total of 24.3 percent of state legislators are women, and eleven women mayors represent only 11 percent of mayors in the hundred largest cities in the nation (topping the list is Mayor Stephanie Rawlings-Blake of Baltimore, Maryland, the fifteenth largest city in the nation, followed by Mayor Ashley Swearengin of Fresno, California, thirty-sixth in the ranking of cities by population). Although women have made tremendous progress in gaining access to positions of political leadership in recent years, they are still "underrepresented at the top and overrepresented at the bottom" in US government at all levels.[4] According to political scientist Susan C. Bourque, public perceptions of women as active participants in the political process are now more common and accepted, yet various societal factors continue to restrict political leadership opportunities for women in the United States. These include the sexual division of labor (women are still predominantly responsible for child care and household chores); differing structures and expectations for the sexes in the workplace (lack of "flex-time" and other career advancement opportunities for women with family responsibilities); ambivalence about women exercising power; and media portrayals of women leaders in a negative light.[5]

■ Women as Political Leaders: Does Gender Matter?

Defining the term *leadership* and determining how it applies to the US political process are essential activities for understanding the unique dynamics within democratic governing institutions. As women continue to gain more prominence as active participants in the US political and electoral process as voters, candidates, and officeholders, it becomes even more important to understand how leadership is defined from a woman's perspective. The essential question becomes, do women political leaders make a difference through their style and approach to governing and policymaking? And, perhaps just as important, how do women differ from each other in leadership positions?

In general terms, *leadership* is defined as the ability to encourage, influence, or inspire others to act in pursuit of a common goal or agenda. How to define such a malleable term like *leadership*, however, is not an easy task. Leadership theories abound that discuss specific traits, skills, styles, or personality characteristics that leaders possess as well as the situations that emerge to allow leaders to then act accordingly.[6] Perhaps one of the most widely recognized theories of leadership would be the work of James MacGregor Burns, who introduced the idea of *transformational leadership* in the late 1970s.[7] For Burns, leadership is more than just the act of wielding power; it involves the relationship between leaders and followers. By way of comparison, he defines *transactional leadership* as the top-down mode of governing that most leaders are able to accomplish—the day-to-day exchanges between leaders and followers that have come to be expected. For example, a congressional candidate may promise to introduce a bill to reform the nation's health care system, and, once elected, may follow through with that plan. Transformational leadership, on the other hand, provides more than just a simple change to a particular policy. A transformational leader provides broader changes to the entire political system that raise the level of motivation and morality in both the leader and the follower. As Burns states, "Transforming leaders define public values that embrace the supreme and enduring principles of a people."[8]

However, as Burns and many other scholars have pointed out, the definition of *leadership* is fluid—it can change based on the context and situation in which the term is used. Although a universal and precise definition of effective or successful leadership may not exist, we do know that historically, leadership has always been defined on male, as opposed to female, terms. In US political, business, and military circles, strong leadership is defined as the ability to exert one's will over a particular situation, and this view has been indoctrinated into the consciousness of most Americans through the traditional interpretation of our national history. This view of leadership, in turn, affects how the public will view other aspiring leaders, particularly women,[9] and it leaves women with a "double standard and a double bind" as men are still more readily accepted as leaders than women.[10] For example, in facing these stereotypes, women leaders are viewed negatively if they exhibit leadership characteristics that are either too masculine (*assertive* translates into being *abrasive*) or too feminine (*soft* translates into *not tough enough to do the job*). Similarly, the term *working mother* carries negative connotations, in that women are perceived as not being able to meet all necessary work responsibilities; meanwhile, the term *working father* is rarely used, as men's child-rearing responsibilities do not enter into the equation.[11] This double bind for women leaders is also due to the fact that gender stereotypes about leadership are both descriptive and prescriptive, meaning that women are expected to be "warm, kind, and sensitive," and if they fail to meet this stereotypical standard, they "may be seen as difficult and unlikable."[12]

This conceptualization of leadership on male terms has often served as a barrier for women in politics—not only those seeking office but those holding it as well. The US policymaking process is viewed as the reallocation of resources throughout society, with the winners exerting their power and influence over the losers within the political arena. Since men are traditionally expected, due to stereotypes, to be competitive, strong, tough, decisive, and in control, male leaders appear to better fit the US political model. Women, by contrast, are expected, again due to stereotypes, to exhibit supportiveness, understanding, and a willingness to both cooperate with and serve others. Other female characteristics of leadership include using consensus decisionmaking, viewing power as something to be shared, encouraging productive approaches to conflict, building supportive working environments, and promoting diversity in the workplace. Gender, socialization, and chosen career paths all play an important role in the defining of leadership and in explanations of the differing leadership styles of women and men.[13]

Scholars who study gender-based differences in leadership show that in some areas, particularly politics and business, women often bring "a more open, democratic, and 'people-centered' approach to their leadership positions." However, a more inclusive and participatory approach to leadership is not exclusive to women, and since women have yet to reach parity with men in leadership positions, not enough evidence yet exists to categorize leadership styles based on gender alone.[14] Differences between male and female leadership styles are sometimes subtle and should not be overstated. It is also important to point out that a "generic woman" does not exist when attempting to determine such differences, because race, class, ethnicity, age, and sexual orientation perhaps play even more important roles when determining the context of one's actions or behaviors in the political arena.[15] And women leaders in other nations have exhibited diverse leadership styles—some more traditionally male, like former British prime minister Margaret Thatcher, and some more traditionally female, like former Philippine president Corazon Aquino.[16]

Does gender matter in the area of policymaking? First, it is important to note that not only is the electoral process in the United States male dominated, but its political institutions are male dominated as well. Once elected, women politicians tend to bring different priorities into the policymaking arena than their male counterparts. Women are also more likely to work across party lines to achieve their goals, as the actions of female members of the US Senate in the past two decades have shown. Both Democratic and Republican women in the Senate have made their collective voices heard on bipartisan issues affecting women, such as the Homemaker Individual Retirement Account (cosponsored by Democrat Barbara Mikulski of Maryland and Republican Kay Bailey Hutchison of Texas, which allows homemakers to invest as much money in tax-free retirement accounts as their working spouses) and a resolution in support of mammograms for women in their forties (cosponsored by Mikulski and Republican Olympia Snowe of Maine).[17]

However, not all women politicians automatically support women's issues, since party affiliation and political ideology are still the most important predictors for bill sponsorship or the actual vote on a particular bill. One study on the state legislatures in California and Arizona showed that there is little difference between the behaviors of male and female members, particularly in regard to meeting the needs of constituents. Whereas women legislators often take the lead on women's issues, both male and female legislators showed a willingness to engage in a cooperative, democratic, and open manner in developing legislation to meet the needs of constituents—even though such willingness is traditionally associated with female leaders.[18] Other studies have shown that although men can easily adopt leadership strategies that are viewed as either male or female, and be praised for doing so, women are viewed more negatively if they adopt more traditionally male leadership style traits such as competitiveness, toughness, or decisiveness.[19]

Women must work hard to survive in the male-dominated world of US politics, particularly in the image-driven, media-saturated political culture that now exists. In 1960, in his study of leadership and the US presidency, Richard Neustadt provided the seminal definition of political power as the ability to effectively bargain and persuade to achieve political objectives.[20] During the television age, that ability to bargain and persuade dictates that politicians must be effective communicators as well as savvy in their dealings with the news media. Therefore, when discussing women and leadership within the US political arena, we must consider the ways in which women communicate, how they are viewed by the public, and how the press portrays them.

Research by communication and linguistics scholars show that men and women communicate differently. In general, men view communication as negotiations where they must maintain power in "a hierarchical social order in which [they are] either one-up or one-down"; women, by contrast, view communication as an opportunity for confirmation, support, and consensus within "a network of connections."[21] This difference can actually benefit women politicians who must appear on television, either during a campaign or while in office. As a medium, television demands intimacy and the ability to express the "private" self; this is obvious in the trend of personalizing politics throughout the 1990s. Male politicians more often discuss goals, whereas women politicians more often reveal themselves through an intimate, conversational, and narrational style of speech. Women politicians tend to be more comfortable expressing as opposed to camouflaging themselves publicly, which can be quite useful in developing their public images.[22]

Negative stereotyping of women politicians, however, can harm that public image. Whether it is positive or negative, stereotyping, which is a method used to quickly categorize information about someone, is a common everyday occurrence. Negative stereotyping about women as ineffective or weak leaders can harm their success as candidates or officeholders. For example, research in recent years has shown stereotypes to exist about both male and female political candidates. Women, who are considered more compassionate, are seen as more competent in the supposedly female policy areas of health care, the environment, education, poverty, and civil rights. Men, who are considered more aggressive, are perceived as being stronger in the supposedly male policy areas of military and defense matters, foreign policy, and economic and trade issues.[23] The portrayal of women as ineffective or weak in these areas can harm their success as candidates or officeholders.

Women in politics, especially those who have succeeded, have also traditionally been viewed by the news media as an anomaly— a unique occurrence that deserves attention because it is outside the norm.[24] Trivialization of women in the news media has also continued, through portrayals on television and in the movies that can lead to "symbolic annihilation" of women in general,[25] as well as the stereotyping that occurs in news coverage of women candidates and politicians.[26] In many campaigns, news media coverage has added to the negative stereotyping of women candidates, thus hurting their efforts to win an elected office, since the news media pay more attention to style over substance when covering female candidates. Many voters may doubt the policy qualifications of women candidates when news coverage downplays issues and highlights personal traits, since this can develop less favorable images of women candidates.[27]

■ **The Plan of the Book**

This text is different than most other women and politics texts in that it looks at the core theme of women and leadership within the US political arena, outlining the essential themes for understanding women and politics from a traditional political science perspective. In addition, I will consider the issue of women's leadership and the challenges associated with the current political environment (the importance of public image, the media, and money) as more women get elected to office (Congress and state governors), appointed to high-ranking federal positions (the executive and judicial branches), and as the United States moves closer to electing the first woman president. We will also consider the impact of women at all levels of the governing process—as citizens, voters, candidates, and office holders—and how, in turn, government policies impact women. For example, how has the government dealt with so-called women's issues (traditionally defined as domestic issues such as welfare, health care, and education) in recent years? Why are certain public policies so important to women and what are the obstacles (if any) to making necessary changes? And, do women politicians bring different perspectives to the policymaking process?

Many students ask, why study women and politics? They also wonder, what is the difference between women and politics and women's studies? Women's studies as an academic discipline grew out of the women's movement in the late 1960s. It began with informal groups of students and professors who were interested in studying gender and asking questions about how women (as opposed to the generic term "man") fit into the political and social order. Since then, and throughout the 1970s and 1980s, the existence of women's and/or gender studies programs has increased dramatically at the college and university level, as has the number of women and politics courses being taught within political science departments across the country. The two areas of study are intricately linked, through the development of feminist theories as well as the methodologies (how we study issues) and core themes of studying women as women (the gendered meanings of social institutions, experiences, events, and ideas). Women's studies courses and programs of study are interdisciplinary, which means that ideas and methodologies come from a variety of disciplines (like political science, history, economics, psychology, philosophy, and communication, to name a few) and are brought together in an attempt to better understand the experiences of women in many facets of life.[28]

Like women's studies, the study of women and politics also grew out of the women's movement. Prior to the late 1960s, as the feminist movement grew within colleges and universities, only a handful of books or studies had ever been conducted about women as political actors. The study of women and politics grew rapidly throughout the 1970s and 1980s, as did the subfield of women and politics within the American Political Science Association. The study of women and politics is more specific than women's studies, focusing solely on women as political participants, officeholders, and policymakers and considering how public policy at all levels of government impacts women. All political scientists, not just those who call themselves women and politics scholars, have benefited from this expansion of disciplinary boundaries by raising questions about what political scientists study and how they study it. By identifying women as a category of study, "feminist political scientists have been able to call into question some of the central assumptions and frameworks of the discipline."[29] However, whereas the discipline of political science "now has gender on its agenda," much research remains to be done to better understand the roles of race, class, party affiliation, and ideology in shaping how women politicians impact the policy-making process, as well as the role of the media in shaping perceptions of women leaders and how that may limit their political opportunities.[30]

This book is firmly grounded within the traditions of women and politics as the field has evolved within political science, and it highlights the theme of political leadership throughout by providing examples and profiles of prominent women political leaders. Understanding the role that women play in US politics must begin with an examination of women as political participants. Chapter 2 provides a historical analysis of the women's movement in the United States and its leaders, including its various phases and its generational differences (for example, the fight for suffrage that culminated in 1920, followed by the drive for an equal rights amendment to the US Constitution that began in 1923 and continued until the amendment's close defeat in 1982). Understanding feminist theory is also relevant to studying women and politics, and this chapter provides a brief discussion of feminist theory and its various classifications (liberal, radical, socialist, Marxist, black, Latina, etc.) and how feminism continues to influence women and politics.

Next, how women participate in politics is examined. Chapter 3 takes a look at women as voters and as members of political parties and interest groups. Important questions include how women vote and why as well as whether there is truly a gender gap in US politics. Also, how do political parties and interest groups represent women's issues, and how do they court women for support? The socialization process, including the role of the news media, is also important to this discussion to determine how women think about politics in general, about their role as voters, and about policy issues relevant to them. Chapter 4 looks at women as political candidates, exploring the unique challenges that women have faced in running for office at all levels of government. Breaking into the system and becoming political leaders are not easy tasks for women candidates, and we will consider the progress that they have made in state and national elections in recent decades. Also, what challenges do women face within the party structure and in raising adequate funds to finance campaigns? Is there gender bias in news media coverage during campaigns, and does this lead to negative stereotyping of women candidates?

The next three chapters will look at women as political leaders, officeholders, and policymakers. Chapter 5 will consider women within Congress and state legislatures. Women holding executive positions at the federal, state, and local levels are covered in Chapter 6; Chapter 7 looks at women within the federal and state judicial branches. To what offices have women been elected and/or appointed, and have they made a difference in the areas of leadership, governance, and policymaking? Have women political leaders effectively raised public awareness of women's policy issues and/or developed workable solutions? Do women governors or legislators govern differently than their male counterparts and/or from one another? What challenges do they face in their careers, and how do these challenges differ from those faced by men? Chapter 6 will also ask a much-talked-about question: when will the United States elect its first woman president?

Finally, Chapter 8 will provide a concluding look at the progress that women have made in US politics, as well as address future challenges for women within the political process as voters, candidates, and political officeholders. Returning to the theme of leadership, we will consider how women impact the political and policymaking process as leaders and what trends may emerge in the future.

■ Study/Discussion Questions

1. Why has leadership traditionally been defined on male, as opposed to female, terms? How has this served as a barrier to women's success in politics?

2. What role did the women's movement have on the academic study of women and gender, particularly within the field of political science?

3. How has the women and politics subfield within political science shaped our understanding of the category "woman"?

■ Online Resources

Center for American Women and Politics, Eagleton Institute of Politics, Rutgers, The State University of New Jersey. http://cawp.rutgers.edu.
50–50 by 2020: Equal Representation in Government. http://www.5050by2020.org.
Women and Politics Research, American Political Science Association. http://www.apsanet.org/~wpol/.

■ **Notes**

1. For example, see Ellison, *If Women Ruled the World;* Rachanow, *If Women Ran the World;* and Rachanow, *What Would You Do If You Ran the World?*
2. Kellerman, "You've Come a Long Way, Baby," 54.
3. Rhode and Kellerman, "Women and Leadership," 1–2.
4. Rhode, ed., "Introduction," 6.
5. Bourque, "Political Leadership for Women," 86–89.
6. See Northouse, *Leadership: Theory and Practice.* Northouse outlines a variety of leadership theories, including those that focus on traits, skills, styles, situations, and personality.
7. See Burns, *Leadership.*
8. Burns, *Transforming Leadership,* 29.
9. Conway, Ahern, and Steuernagel, *Women and Political Participation,* 112.
10. Rhode and Kellerman, "Women and Leadership," 7.
11. Ibid., 7–8.
12. Carli and Eagly, "Overcoming Resistance to Women Leaders," 128.
13. See Hoyt, "Women and Leadership," 265–292.
14. Stapleton, "Introduction," 33.
15. Rhode, "Introduction," 5.
16. Genovese, "Women as National Leaders," 214–215.
17. Whitney et al., *Nine and Counting,* 125–127.
18. Reingold, *Representing Women,* 243.
19. Freeman and Bourque, "Leadership and Power," 8–9.
20. See Neustadt, *Presidential Power and the Modern Presidents.*
21. Tannen, *You Just Don't Understand,* 24–25.
22. Jamieson, *Beyond the Double Bind,* 94–95.
23. See Huddy and Terkildsen, "Gender Stereotypes."
24. Rice, "Women Out of the Myths and into Focus," 45–49.
25. See Tuchman, *Hearth and Home,* 7–8, and Paletz, *The Media in American Politics,* 135–139.
26. See Braden, *Women Politicians and the Media.*
27. Kahn, *The Political Consequences of Being a Woman,* 134–136.
28. Sapiro, *Women in American Society,* 7–10.
29. See Carroll and Zerilli, "Feminist Challenges to Political Science."
30. Bourque, "Political Leadership for Women," 106.

2

The Women's Movement and Feminism in the United States

The true republic: men, their rights, and nothing more; women, their rights, and nothing less.
■ Motto of the weekly newspaper *The Revolution*, edited by Susan B. Anthony

The women's movement in America, which entered its third century with the arrival of the new millennium in 2001, has had many highs and lows along the way. Although many political victories have been achieved, like gaining suffrage during the early part of the twentieth century, the women's movement has also experienced its share of setbacks, like the defeat of the Equal Rights Amendment (ERA) to the US Constitution in 1982. And it is especially important to note that not all women have been a part of the women's movement in the United States, nor have all agreed with the various policy changes that the movement has sought regarding a woman's public role. In general, the women's movement has sought the breakdown of what are known as the public and private spheres, which had been the traditional way of life for men and women since the earliest days of the US colonies; the home was a woman's domain, while public matters, including those of government and politics, were the sole responsibility of men. As a result, women had no public voice, and in most cases they were not viewed as equal citizens in the eyes of the law.

From the start, those who affiliated themselves with the women's movement sought more equality and fairness for women as well as an end to the patriarchal treatment of women in all aspects of their lives. While there are many historical moments that have shaped the women's movement, as well as different policy outcomes that have been sought by the movement's various leaders, some common interests have survived the test of time. According to political scientist Anne N. Costain, "Throughout their long history, women's movements, whether labeled suffrage, temperance, women's liberation, or antislavery, are linked in their consistent cry for democratic inclusion—politically, economically, educationally, and in the professions."[1]

Although this chapter is not meant to analyze every aspect of the history of the women's rights movement in America, it will highlight the broadly defined phases or "waves" of the women's movement as well as a few of the prominent women leaders who shaped the cause. The first wave is generally considered the fight for women's suffrage, beginning in 1848 at the Seneca Falls Convention and culminating in 1920 with the passage of the Nineteenth Amendment to the US Constitution, which granted women the right to vote. The second wave of the women's movement emerged in the politically turbulent decade of the 1960s and coincided in part with the civil rights movement, with major attention focused on breaking down the legal barriers to sexual equality and, toward the end of this period, on the failed passage of the ERA. However, this second wave is known for a narrow view of women's rights as held by mostly middle- and upper-class white women. The third wave of the women's rights movement began in the 1990s and has focused on increased political participation by women as well as a more inclusive notion of women's rights to include the concerns of racial, ethnic, and gender minorities. In addition to history, we will also consider the basic categories of feminist theory and how feminism continues to influence women as political leaders.

▪ The First Wave of the US Women's Movement

Throughout our nation's history, women have struggled with the issue of the public versus private spheres—that is, with the fact that men controlled the public sphere while women were relegated to the household and child-rearing chores in the private/domestic sphere. Despite all the talk of liberty and of all men being created equal during the revolutionary period, women in the US colonies were confined to domestic duties and had few legal rights. They could not vote or hold public office; few had any kind of formal education, and divorce was difficult to obtain. In several colonies, married women could not own property and had no legal rights over their children.

However, "the revolutionary ferment offered women new opportunities and engendered in many a new outlook" as they began to aid the war effort and help the US armies in their fight against the British by raising money, plowing fields, making ammunitions, and cooking, cleaning, and caring for the soldiers.[2] While most women remained in the private sphere during this era, a few outspoken women began to demand equal treatment during and after the war. As early as 1776, Abigail Adams, wife of John Adams and future first lady, wrote to her husband with her now-famous demand for equality:

> I long to hear that you have declared an independency—and by the way in the new Code of Laws which I suppose it will be necessary for you to make I desire you would Remember the Ladies, and be more generous and favourable to them than your ancestors. Do not put such unlimited power into the hands of the Husbands. Remember all Men would be tyrants if they could. If perticular care and attention is not paid to the Ladies we are determined to foment a Rebellion, and will not hold ourselves bound by any Laws in which we have no voice, or Representation.[3]

Unfortunately, John Adams and the other eventual framers of the Constitution were not to be persuaded, and the legal status of women did not improve after the American Revolution or with the ratification of the US Constitution in 1789 or the Bill of Rights in 1791. The rights of women were not addressed in the documents, and, "by today's standards, it is impossible to deny that the original Constitution was a racist and sexist document or that the Framers wrote it in a way that benefited them."[4] As the United States moved into the nineteenth century and as the nation began to experience rapid industrialization that moved the economy away from its agrarian roots, the "cult of domesticity" took a stronger cultural hold on women. The home became a safe haven from the cruel world outside, and it was the responsibility of women to civilize their husbands and children. It also became an accepted social norm that "men and women were designed by God and nature to inhabit 'separate spheres.'"[5] Legal and political rights for women remained much as they had been in the colonial era, with no right to vote and little or no control over property or custody of children.

The formal women's rights movement began in 1848 at the Seneca Falls Convention, convened by Lucretia Mott and Elizabeth Cady Stanton. Most women who attended had been active in the abolitionist movement for years, even decades. The idea for the convention had been born following the 1840 World Anti-Slavery Convention in London, where female delegates, including Mott and Stanton, had not been allowed to participate and were even forced to sit behind a partition so as not to be seen. Prior to the Seneca Falls Convention, Stanton wrote her famous Declaration of Sentiments and Resolutions, a bold document declaring the rights of women modeled after the Declaration of Independence. In it, Stanton demanded economic and property rights and denounced many accepted practices of the time, including slavery, discrimination in education, the exploitation of women in the workforce, the patriarchal family, and divorce and child custody laws; she also denounced organized religion as "perpetuating women's oppression." Although suffrage would become the major issue of the latter stages of the first wave of the women's movement, it was not at Seneca Falls:

> Popular belief has it that the nineteenth-century movement focused solely on suffrage, but that became true only in the movement's later, diluted form. At Seneca Falls, the demand for suffrage was almost an afterthought, a last-minute item Stanton tacked on to the list—the only resolution not unanimously supported. In fact, at its inception, this movement was radical and multi-issued. It named male power over women "absolute tyranny."[6]

Yet securing the right to vote did emerge as the major issue for the movement, since women's activists like Stanton, Alice Paul, and Susan B. Anthony believed suffrage to be the most effective way to gain access to the political system and change the unjust way that women were viewed in the eyes of the law. They also eventually realized that slavery would end and that all men regardless of race—but not women—would be given the right to vote following the passage of the Thirteenth, Fourteenth, and

Fifteenth Amendments to the Constitution (in 1865, 1868, and 1870, respectively). Thus, a nearly seventy-five-year struggle ensued to earn the right for women to vote. Many of the leaders of the women's movement had gained leadership and organizational skills as activists in the abolitionist movement, so for many generations of suffragists the strategy to achieve what at the time seemed like a radical change to the Constitution included protests, marches, lectures, writings, and various forms of civil disobedience.

From the start, Stanton and Anthony were prominent leaders within the suffrage movement. Both had been active in the American Equal Rights Association (AERA), which had been formed in 1866 to fight for universal suffrage. However, the organization disbanded in 1869 due to internal conflicts involving the political priorities of the group, which was split as to whether women's suffrage should be a higher priority than black male suffrage. In May 1869, Stanton and Anthony formed the National Woman Suffrage Association (NWSA, which would eventually become the League of Women Voters in the 1920s and is still in existence today). Led by Anthony, the NWSA preferred fighting for a constitutional amendment to give women the right to vote nationally. A second group, the American Woman Suffrage Association (AWSA), was formed in November 1869 by Lucy Stone and Henry Blackwell to fight for suffrage on a state-by-state basis. Anthony had gained national attention as well as much-needed support for advocating a constitutional amendment to give women the vote when she was arrested and tried for voting in the 1872 presidential election. The amendment, first introduced in Congress in 1878, was presented to forty consecutive sessions of Congress until it finally passed as a proposed amendment in 1919.[7]

Along the way, the suffrage movement faced fierce opposition from a variety of groups. Big business (particularly the liquor industry), the Catholic Church, and political machine bosses feared that women voters would support political reform. Women led many of the temperance efforts of the late nineteenth and early twentieth centuries in an attempt to ban the sale of alcohol. Other organizations, like the National Consumer's League, formed in 1899, and the National Women's Trade Union League, formed in 1903, worked to change labor conditions for various corporations. Leaders in many southern states also opposed

women's suffrage because they did not want African American
women to gain access to voting rights or because they believed
that suffrage was a state, not a federal, issue.[8] Just as they did in
the suffrage movement, women emerged as strong leaders in the
antisuffrage movement. The women leaders in both movements
tended to be among the social elite—educated, with access to
money and important social contacts. But many women did not
support the breakdown of the dichotomy between the public and
private spheres, fearing that they would lose their power and
influence within the domestic sphere and among their social networks if forced to become participants in public life. It is important to remember that neither women's suffrage nor other causes
of the women's movement universally concerned all women, as we
will discuss later in this chapter.

Between 1878 and August 1920, when the Nineteenth
Amendment was ratified, activists for women's voting rights relied
on a variety of strategies to gain support for the proposed amendment. Legal strategies were used in an attempt to invalidate male-
only voting laws, while others sought to pass suffrage laws at the
state level. Some women fighting for the cause could not be
deterred, enduring hunger strikes, staging rallies and vote-ins, and
even being jailed for publicly campaigning for the amendment.
The movement became revitalized with an influx of younger
women joining the fight in 1910 due to immigration, urbaniza-
tion, and an expanding female labor force; the cause also won a
state referendum in Washington granting women the right to vote
that same year. California would follow in 1911, and by 1912, a
total of nine western states had passed legislation giving women
the right to vote. (As a territory, Wyoming had granted women
full suffrage in 1869, and it retained the law when it became a
state in 1890. The other six western states included Colorado,
Utah, Idaho, Arizona, Kansas, and Oregon.)

Another major turning point came in 1916 when a coalition of
suffrage organizations, temperance groups, women's social welfare
organizations, and reform-minded politicians pooled their efforts
and resources to wage a fiercer public battle. The political tide
began to turn in the suffragists' favor in 1917, when New York
adopted women's suffrage legislation. Then, in 1918, President
Woodrow Wilson also changed his position and backed the constitutional amendment. On May 21, 1919, the House of
Representatives passed the proposed amendment, followed by the

Senate two weeks later. Tennessee became the thirty-sixth state to ratify the amendment on August 18, 1920, which gave it the necessary three-fourths support from the states; it was officially certified by Secretary of State Bainbridge Colby eight days later on August 26, 1920. Few of the early supporters for women's suffrage, including Anthony and Stanton, lived to see the final political victory.

In the immediate postsuffrage era, several women's rights activists, including Carrie Chapman Catt and Alice Paul, sought to capitalize on the momentum of finally receiving the vote and began to lobby Congress for an Equal Rights Amendment to the Constitution. Catt, a leader of the suffrage movement, had served as president of the National American Woman Suffrage Association (NAWSA, which was formed in 1890 when the NWSA and AWSA had merged) from 1900 to 1904 and again from 1915 until ratification of the Nineteenth Amendment in 1920. Catt then founded the League of Women Voters that same year. Paul had been instrumental in pushing the suffrage cause to victory as head of NAWSA's Congressional Committee but left the organization in 1913 to form the Congressional Union for Woman Suffrage, which became the National Women's Party in 1917. In 1923, Paul drafted the ERA and the National Women's Party presented it to Congress. From that year onward, Congress annually considered various versions of an ERA, yet never passed a constitutional amendment for the states to consider. (To amend the US Constitution, a two-thirds vote is necessary in both the House of Representatives and the Senate to propose the amendment for consideration by the states. For ratification, three-fourths of the states, thirty-eight of fifty, must approve the amendment.) Finally, in 1972, after intense lobbying by groups such as the National Organization for Women (NOW) and Business and Professional Women (BPW), Congress passed the proposed ERA. The contents of the proposed amendment were brief and to the point:

> Section 1. Equality of rights under the law shall not be denied or abridged by the United States or by any State on account of sex.
>
> Section 2. The Congress shall have the power to enforce, by appropriate legislation, the provisions of this article.
>
> Section 3. The Amendment shall take effect two years after the date of ratification.

By 1973, twenty-two states had ratified the amendment, but by the initial deadline of 1978, only thirty-five states had signed on for ratification. In spite of an extended deadline to 1982, momentum for passage faltered under intense opposition from religious groups such as the National Council of Catholic Women and the Mormon Church, as well as political groups opposed to the ERA such as the Eagle Forum, led by Phyllis Schlafly. Many observers have noted that the ERA "divided rather than united women politically and culturally."[9] Not only were women divided over whether or not to support the amendment, various opinions existed as to whether it would really make a difference in terms of legal rights for women. Some argued that the amendment was merely symbolic, while others feared that passage would do away with various legal protections for women in the workplace, as well as those involving child support and exemption from military registration.

After the initial excitement of the proposed constitutional amendment, public support and political enthusiasm waned in the years leading up to the deadline set for 1982. Although passage of the amendment would have been a political victory for the women's rights movement, many of the gender-based classifications that ERA supporters hoped to outlaw had already been changed through Supreme Court rulings, legislation in Congress, and presidential executive orders. According to political scientist Jane J. Mansbridge, the defeat of the amendment was not all that surprising: "[T]he puzzle is not why the ERA died but why it came so close to passing. . . . The irony in all this is that the ERA would have had much less substantive effect than either proponents or opponents claimed."[10] Yet the ERA remained a prominent rallying call for the feminist leaders of the second wave of the women's movement.

■ The Second Wave and the Modern Women's Movement

Although the fight for the ERA certainly played an important role in the modern women's movement, several other issues began to take center stage for US women throughout the 1960s as the movement entered its second wave. With similarities to the civil rights movement throughout the decade, the mainstream women's rights

Failure Is Impossible: The Political Leadership of Elizabeth Cady Stanton and Susan B. Anthony

In the early women's rights movement in the United States, perhaps no two women were as influential as Elizabeth Cady Stanton and Susan B. Anthony. And due to the lasting partnership that the two developed in pursuing women's rights and women's suffrage, one's contribution to the cause cannot be discussed without also considering the contributions of the other. Each had unique leadership strengths that seemed to perfectly complement the other; in the words of Judith E. Harper, "Stanton was the leading voice and philosopher of the women's rights and suffrage movements, while Anthony was the powerhouse who commandeered the legions of women who struggled to win the ballot for American women."[11] Stanton and Anthony also exemplify what political scientist Bruce Miroff calls *dissenting leadership,* a model of leadership for a group that was "denied the fundamental rights of citizenship and was excluded from participation in public life."[12]

Stanton (1815–1902) is known as the founding mother of feminism and the "boldest and most brilliant leader of the feminist movement in nineteenth-century America."[13] The wife of prominent abolitionist Henry Stanton and a mother of seven, Stanton was thirty-two years old when she helped to convene the Seneca Falls Convention in 1848. A graduate of Troy Female Seminary, she refused to be merely what she called a "household drudge"; when she and Henry married, the word "obey" was omitted from the ceremony. They honeymooned in London while attending the World Anti-Slavery Convention in 1840. After her call for a woman's right to vote at Seneca Falls, Stanton was opposed by fellow organizer Lucretia Mott as well as by her own husband, both of whom thought the idea was too radical. Soon after, in 1850, Stanton would meet and develop a lifelong friendship with Susan B. Anthony, who would join in Stanton's cause for women's rights and women's suffrage. In 1866, Stanton became the first woman ever to run for the House of Representatives when she realized that although New York state law prohibited women from voting, it did not prohibit them from running for or holding public office. Her election bid was unsuccessful.

Susan B. Anthony (1820–1906) became a teacher at the age of seventeen. After teaching for fifteen years, she became active in the temperance movement, considered one of the first expressions of

continues

Failure Is Impossible *continued*

American feminism insofar as it dealt with the abuse of women and children at the hands of alcoholic husbands and fathers. As a woman, however, Anthony was not allowed to speak at public rallies. As a result, she helped to found the Woman's State Temperance Society of New York, one of the first women's associations of its kind. Soon after meeting Stanton in 1850, she joined the women's rights movement and dedicated her life to achieving suffrage for women. Unlike Stanton, Anthony never married and did not have the burden of raising children. As a result, she focused her attention on organization within the movement, and was more often the one who traveled, lectured, and canvassed nationwide for suffrage. She was arrested for attempting to vote on more than one occasion beginning in 1872, but remained committed to her campaign for a constitutional amendment allowing women the right to vote. In 1900, Anthony persuaded the University of Rochester to admit women, and she remained an active lecturer and activist for the cause of suffrage until her death.

Together, Stanton and Anthony formed the Women's Loyal National League in 1863 in New York City to demand the end of slavery. In 1868, they founded the Workingwoman's Association, which sought to improve working conditions for women, and also started a weekly newspaper aptly named *The Revolution*, which demanded, among other things, equal pay for women. The following year, they founded the National Woman Suffrage Association in search of a more radical solution than had been proposed by the American Equal Rights Association. Stanton would serve as president of the organization for twenty-one years, in spite of the fact that she differed with Anthony's view of the need for suffrage to be the single issue dominating the woman's rights movement. Stanton, "known for her searching intellect, wide-ranging views, and radical positions," is remembered as the "preeminent women's rights theorist of nineteenth-century America."[14] Anthony, who became the first woman to have her image appear on any form of US currency with the Susan B. Anthony dollar's debut in 1979, is remembered as the woman most identified with women's suffrage and the passage of the Nineteenth Amendment.[15] Together, their early brand of political leadership shaped the lives of millions of US women.

movement turned its attention to ending the cult of domesticity that had been the ideal during the 1950s. Women had made great progress during the 1940s in the workforce during World War II, when millions of US men served in the military, leaving a variety of jobs open for women. However, many of those women who had experienced professional success and were seen as patriots by helping out the US economy during the war were displaced from their jobs when the soldiers returned home. The start of the postwar baby boom era in the late 1940s, coupled with the new trend of suburbanization across the nation, left the lives of most US women once again dominated by responsibilities in the private sphere.

The publication of Betty Friedan's book *The Feminine Mystique* became one of the most important events for the women's rights movement in the early 1960s. A 1942 graduate of Smith College, Friedan had spent ten years as a suburban New York wife and mother doing occasional freelance writing when she circulated a questionnaire among her Smith classmates in 1957 to determine their satisfaction with their lives. When she discovered that they were resoundingly not satisfied with their life experiences as wives and mothers, Friedan embarked on a much more intensive analysis using her undergraduate training in psychology, which resulted in the publication of *The Feminine Mystique* in 1963. The book immediately struck a chord with millions of women who shared Friedan's view that they were trapped in the supposed domestic bliss of hearth and home and that they had no real identity, simply living vicariously through their husbands and children. The book became an immediate, yet controversial, best seller. Describing "the problem that has no name," Friedan wrote:

> Virtually every powerful cultural institution—magazines, television, advice books, schools, and religious leaders—prescribed a middle-class ideal for women: they were to be wives and mothers, nothing more, nothing less. . . . Suburbs gave a new, geographic twist to the old split between private and public, family and work, personal and political. The work suburban women actually did, inventing new forms of creative motherhood and elaborating networks of volunteer institutions, was not seen as, well, *real* work.[16]

The response that Friedan received from thousands of letters written by women from various social backgrounds, telling the author that the book had changed their lives, convinced her that a new chapter in the women's movement had been born. And although she had not originally sought such a position, Friedan became the leader of this new wave of the movement. Taking this new leadership role seriously, she began touring the country to talk about practical solutions to some of the problems that women, particularly in the workforce, were facing, such as the lack of affordable day care, flexible work schedules, or maternity leaves to accommodate family needs. Inspired by the civil rights movement, Friedan declared the need for a "women's NAACP." In October 1966, she cofounded the National Organization for Women (NOW), a civil rights group dedicated to achieving equality for women in US society. As NOW's first president, a post she held until 1970, Friedan lobbied for an end to sex-classified employment notices as well as for greater representation of women in political office, child care centers for working mothers, legalized abortion, and other political reforms. In 1969, she became a founding member of the National Abortion Rights Action League (NARAL), and in 1971 she also became a founding member of the National Women's Political Caucus (discussed in Chapter 5). Throughout the 1970s and early 1980s, Friedan also worked as an outspoken proponent for passage of the ERA.[17]

Membership in NOW and other women's organizations grew rapidly during the early 1970s as the women's rights movement capitalized on the political momentum first started a decade earlier. President John F. Kennedy had formed the Commission on the Status of Women in 1961 in response to concerns about women's equality, and, based on the commission's various studies at both the national and state levels that showed pay inequity based on sex, Congress passed the Equal Pay Act in 1963. Other political victories for sexual equality came within the decade, for instance, Congress's 1972 passage of the Equal Rights Amendment for ratification and of Title IX of the Educational Amendments Act that same year, which required equal opportunity for women in all aspects of education, including admissions, financial aid, and funding for women's athletic programs. And in 1973, the Supreme Court, ruling on *Roe v. Wade*, struck down state laws banning abortion in the first three months of pregnancy. Advocates for women's rights saw the decision as a major victory, since reproductive rights and the ability of women to control their own bodies were on the forefront of their political agenda.

But not all US women were on board with this new wave of the women's rights movement, and not all believed in the causes supported by Friedan and other prominent feminists at that time such as Gloria Steinem (to be discussed), Susan Brownmiller (an early organizer of this phase of the women's movement and best-selling feminist author), and Flo Kennedy (an attorney and civil rights/women's rights activist who was also the first black woman to graduate from Columbia Law School). Despite the changing workforce in the United States, where a two-income family became the norm throughout the 1970s and 1980s, many working women did not consider themselves feminists. The victory for prochoice feminists in legalizing abortion also galvanized the pro-life movement at the national level, and those organizations opposed to passage of the ERA also gained national prominence. Under the leadership of Phyllis Schlafly, the Eagle Forum, founded in 1972, fought to stop passage of the ERA and to protect what its members believed to be traditional family values and the traditional role of women in society, which they considered under attack by feminists. Another group, Concerned Women for America (CWA), also became a prominent antifeminist and anti-ERA group. Founded in 1979 by Beverly LaHaye, the wife of fundamentalist Baptist minister and Moral Majority cofounder Tim LaHaye, the mission of CWA was to promote biblical values in all areas of public policy. Both organizations are still in existence. The formation of these groups in response to the women's rights agenda shows the diversity of viewpoints, even in the 1970s, about a woman's role in society. As historian Ruth Rosen points out, "Insecure in their separate worlds, women privately sniped at each other: housewives blasted activists as unpatriotic; working women derided housewives as spoiled and lazy; and housewives accused working women of neglecting their children."[18]

Divisions even emerged within the women's movement, as more moderate feminists (who tended to represent the view of middle- to upper-class white women) clashed with more radical feminists (who wanted to broaden the movement beyond the pursuit of legal equality to bring about more radical change for women within all aspects of society). By the 1980s, the women's rights movement had succeeded in bringing about many legisla-

Gloria Steinem: Feminist Leader and Cultural Icon

Known as a feminist leader, journalist, best-selling author, and social activist, Gloria Steinem has been one of the most enduring forces within the women's movement since the 1960s. Now that she is in her seventies, there are not many parts of Steinem's life that have not become part of the public dialogue about feminism and the women's movement. Her celebrity status and her desire to remain unconventional have also kept her in the news for decades; from the early days of the modern women's movement, the fact that she was physically attractive defied the media stereotype of feminists. Early in her career as a freelance journalist, she infiltrated New York's Playboy Club as an undercover "bunny" to write an expose about how women employees were sexually harassed and discriminated against there. She went public with the fact that she had had an abortion in the 1950s while she was in college, a time when the procedure was still illegal in the United States. She had a four-year relationship with Mort Zuckerman, the conservative publisher of *U.S. News and World Report*, and once had to deny a relationship with former Secretary of State Henry Kissinger after they were photographed together in public. In 2000 she made headlines again when, at the age of sixty-six, she married for the first time (an institution she had long railed against as destroying a woman's identity and as an "arrangement for one-and-a-half people").

In terms of her political accomplishments, Steinem was among the leaders of the women's rights movement in the late 1960s and early 1970s in the campaigns for reproductive rights, equal pay and equal representation, and an end to domestic violence. She helped to found the National Women's Political Caucus in 1971, as well as the groundbreaking *Ms. Magazine* and the Ms. Foundation for Women in 1972. She is also a founding member of the Coalition of Labor Union Women, and her books, *Outrageous Acts and Everyday Rebellions* (1983) and *Revolution from Within: A Book of Self-Esteem* (1992), are best sellers. When *Ms. Magazine* first appeared as a one-time insert in *New York Magazine* in December 1971, no one gave a magazine dedicated to women's rights and feminist views a chance for survival against the traditional women's magazines that gave "advice about saving marriages, raising babies, or using the right cosmetics." But the 300,000 test copies sold out nationwide in only eight days, generating 26,000 subscription

continues

Gloria Steinem *continued*

orders. According to the *Ms.* Web page, "few realized it would become the landmark institution in both women's rights and American journalism that it is today. . . . [And it] was the first national magazine to make feminist voices audible, feminist journalism tenable, and a feminist worldview available to the public."[19] The magazine's success and ability to survive for three decades is even more impressive given the fact that it has remained free of advertising for most of its existence. Steinem has been involved with the magazine, whether as an editor or a writer, for all but a few years of its publication.

Steinem is also known for her compelling, and sometimes controversial, quotes about how women have been treated in US society. Among the most notable are "if the shoe doesn't fit, must we change the foot?" and "a woman without a man is like a fish without a bicycle" (the latter actually coined by Australian author Irina Dunn, but often attributed to Steinem as well). Steinem continues to speak out about feminist issues and causes and acknowledges the many changes the women's movement has undergone since the 1960s. Whereas women of her generation rebelled against the pressures to marry, have children, take their husband's names, and be the picture of supposed femininity, Steinem acknowledges that many women in the twenty-first century embrace the traditional notion of being a wife and mother, but that women now have the choice to devote their lives to family, career, or both. In a January 2005 interview, she stated that whereas being a wife and mother are no longer "social imperatives" like they were several decades ago, the women's movement is no way diminished and is still necessary: "It's like saying, 'We're living in a post-democracy.' It's ridiculous. We've hardly begun. The good news is that [US] feminism used to be three crazy women in New York: now a third of the country self-identify as feminists, and 60 percent if you go by the dictionary definition."[20] Clearly, the debate over feminism and the women's movement lives on.

tive changes that granted equality to women, despite the failure of the ERA. Yet the debate over the role of women in US society would continue into the 1990s and beyond as a younger generation of feminists weighed in on where the women's rights movement had been and where it should go in the future.

■ **The Third Wave: Generation X and Beyond**

By 1990, many political observers believed that feminism in the
United States was dead. But according to women's studies scholar
Astrid Henry, the publication of two key books in 1991—*Backlash:
The Undeclared War on American Women* by Susan Faludi and *The
Beauty Myth: How Images of Beauty Are Used Against Women* by
Naomi Wolf—began to challenge the idea that the women's
movement was over. Both Faludi and Wolf represented a "new
generation of popular feminist writing" that helped to reinvigo-
rate interest in the women's movement.[21] Faludi wrote about how
the gains, both political and legal, made by women during the
1970s had been followed by a backlash during the 1980s, a decade
in which a conservative Republican—President Ronald Reagan—
dominated the political environment. Wolf pointed out some of
the key differences in the women's movement by generation, since
those who had fought the battles in the heyday of the second wave
did not necessarily represent the attitudes and beliefs of younger
feminists. Other events during this time period also contributed
to the renewed public interest in women's issues, including the
Supreme Court confirmation hearing of Clarence Thomas in the
fall of 1991 as well as the increased number of women running for
public office in 1992 (as we will discuss in Chapters 4 and 5).
Images of strong women were suddenly prominent in Hollywood
as well with the release of the movie *Thelma & Louise* in 1991
(about two women fighting back against male violence, which
grossed more than US$45 million) and the popularity of two top-
rated sitcoms starring women—ABC's *Roseanne* (named for the
star of the show, Roseanne Barr, who portrayed a strong-willed
mother in a working-class family in a small midwestern town) and
CBS's *Murphy Brown* (starring Candice Bergen as a single and successful forty-something political reporter on a television network
news show in Washington, D.C.).[22]

What is now referred to as the third wave of the women's
movement got its start in the political and social environment of
the early 1990s. Unlike the second wave of the women's movement, which largely focused on equality and the inclusion of
women in traditionally male-dominated areas, the third wave (also
known as postfeminism) continues to challenge and expand common definitions of gender and sexuality. The third wave, which

represents those feminists born between 1965 and 1976 (Generation X) and from 1977 to 1997 (Generation Y), also seeks to move beyond the political battles—equal access to work, education, and athletics—that the older generation of feminists had fought before them. This wave of the movement reflects the unique views of women's issues and feminism held by the generation of women who came of age mostly in the 1980s, when feminism had already been a part of the world in which they grew up. Third-wave Generation X feminists began moving beyond the monolithic, white, middle-class views of earlier feminists to embrace a more multicultural view that included women of all races, ethnicities, and socioeconomic backgrounds. Not only has a more global view of women's issues emerged, but a common theme is found in the prowoman emphasis on personal empowerment, as opposed to the anti-man stereotype that became part of the image of feminists in the late 1980s and early 1990s.[23] The difference between the two generations, according to Henry, remains a crucial part of the identity of third-wave feminists: "This refused identification, or disidentification, is frequently with or against second-wave feminism. . . . [F]or many younger feminists, it is only by refusing to identify themselves with earlier versions of feminism—and frequently with older feminists—that they are able to create a feminism of their own."[24]

Today's younger feminists are also called "stealth feminists," due to the media's backlash of painting the women's movement in a negative light. Until the early 1990s, the media kept talking about the end of feminism, yet younger generations of women began reshaping the movement with various articles and books about the third-wave agenda.[25] As Debra Michaels puts it:

> Beyond endless accounts of young women from so-called Generations X, Y, and Z renouncing feminism with the oft-repeated, "I'm not a feminist, but . . . ," lay another reality: countless thirty-something women not only embracing the label but defining our lives as torchbearers for feminism. In our careers, relationships, child-raising strategies (or decisions not to have children)—in all our choices—"Stealth Feminists" have been quietly, invisibly, and sometimes even subconsciously continuing the work of the Women's Movement.[26]

Prominent third-wave authors include Jennifer Baumgardner and Amy Richards, who point out that many women of their generation take women's rights and feminism for granted, which causes one of the biggest challenges for the movement: "[F]or anyone born after the early 1960s. . . . feminism is like fluoride. We scarcely notice that we have it—it's simply in the water."[27]

Politically, the third wave of the women's movement has also focused on candidate recruitment, campaign resources, more public roles for women, and grassroots political activism. Their agenda has also included the issues associated with the economically disadvantaged as well as with racial, ethnic, and gender minorities. There is a strong link to the Democratic Party, particularly during President Bill Clinton's administration as "softer" women's issues came to the forefront during the economic prosperity of the 1990s, including education, family, jobs, and health care. At the start of the 1990s, national security took a back seat in the national debate with the end of the Cold War. Following the terrorist attacks of September 11, 2001, the national debate would again change, with national security issues eclipsing domestic issues. This, along with a trend supporting conservative Republican victories in Congress (in 1994) and the White House (in 2000) made the pursuit of the third-wave agenda on the national level more challenging for feminist leaders.[28] However, many of these domestic policy issues reemerged in the national agenda—including health care, job creation, a minimum-wage increase, and environmental issues—after the Democratic Party won control of both houses of Congress in 2006 and President Barack Obama was elected in 2008.

Concurrent with the third wave of feminism has also been the growing political power of conservative women's groups and activists opposed to the feminist agenda. With a conservative Republican majority in Congress from 1995 to 2007, and a conservative Republican president in the White House from 2001 to 2009, groups such as the CWA and the Independent Women's Forum (IWF) became key players in policy debates by "articulating alternative bases for understanding women's political interests." Although both groups promote various conservative viewpoints and policies, the CWA maintains its Christian-based philosophy to promote the causes of social conservatives whereas the IWF (which was formed in 1992 by women who had organized in 1991 to support the Supreme Court nomination of Clarence Thomas) consists of professional women with an eco-

Rebecca Walker: Leading the Third Wave

A leader of the third-wave feminist movement, award-winning author Rebecca Walker is one of the most prominent voices of feminism in the United States today. After graduating from Yale University with honors in 1992, Walker cofounded the Third Wave Foundation, a nonprofit organization dedicated to working with young women and transgender youths aged from fifteen to thirty to become active citizens and leaders in pursuit of social justice. Considered a superstar among third-wave feminists, Walker edited her first book—*To Be Real: Telling the Truth and Changing the Face of Feminism*—in 1995, thereby helping to solidify the emerging view of younger feminists as more inclusive of different perspectives and life experiences than the women's rights activists of the 1960s and 1970s. Walker, however, has strong family ties to the second wave of feminism; her mother is feminist author and activist Alice Walker, who won the Pulitzer Prize for the novel *The Color Purple* in 1983, and her godmother is Gloria Steinem. Since 1995, Walker has written three other books and regularly contributes to major US newspapers and magazines, appears on major news programs, and has been a contributing editor to *Ms. Magazine* since 1989.

Due to her personal history and her decision to write about many facets of her life in her books, Walker seems to stand at the intersections of race, ethnicity, and gender that are so prominent in third-wave feminism. In her 2001 book *Black, White, and Jewish: Autobiography of a Shifting Self,* she writes about growing up with a black mother and a Jewish father, as well as about her sexual relationships with both men and women. But just as there is no monolithic definition of feminism, Walker's views as a feminist have continued to evolve. Viewed by some as a radical feminist, Walker challenged that image with her 2007 book *Baby Love: Choosing Motherhood After a Lifetime of Ambivalence*, which tackles the topic of work versus motherhood and the related challenges still facing younger women. She wrote the book after giving birth to her own child while in a committed relationship with the child's father. Other prominent third-wave feminists such as Jennifer Baumgardner view Walker's evolving views on topics such as pregnancy and motherhood as a "contribution to the Third Wave sensibility, not a betrayal of it."[29]

Walker, who regularly lectures at colleges and universities,

continues

Rebecca Walker *continued*

continues to promote the need for acceptance and inclusion within feminism and feminist causes. In 2008, when Sarah Palin's selection as the Republican vice presidential candidate became a flashpoint for feminists—raising the question of whether a conservative, prolife candidate could represent a different brand of feminism—Walker defended Palin as a symbol of female empowerment despite disagreeing with her on numerous policy positions. Writing for *The Huffington Post* in September 2008, Walker also discussed how "Palin Power" was a product of "conservatives exploiting the breach created by feminist leadership." She recalled the recent backlash against her own views by other feminists protesting her insistence "on the necessity of intergenerational power sharing within feminist institutions, the full integration of men into organizations working for gender parity, and the necessity of finding commonality with women who don't hold progressive views. In response, I've been attacked, undermined, and politically abused by some of the very women I sought to serve." Walker also recalled a talk she gave to the National Women's Studies Association a few years prior, wherein she urged members "to be more open, more tolerant, and more inclusive of women and men who do not share a progressive agenda." Her remarks were perceived as both controversial and inappropriate.[30] Walker's writings and leadership within the feminist movement are a reminder of how far feminism has evolved since the 1960s, and how for many, that evolution is far from over.

nomically conservative approach toward public policies. According to political scientist Ronnee Schreiber, these two groups now play a significant role in the public dialogue and offer a legitimate view of women's issues: "As women's political power has increased, so too has a contest among national organizations fighting to represent women's interests in the policymaking process. Although feminists have long dominated the political landscape in terms of numbers and visibility, they are increasingly being challenged by other national organizations—those that are antifeminist and also claim to represent women's interests. These conservative women's groups present a substantial threat to the feminist movement."[31]

■ **Feminisms and US Politics**

There is no simple or single definition for the word *feminism*. First used by women fighting for suffrage in the United States at the turn of the twentieth century, the term was more broadly used by the women's movement in the 1970s in an attempt to bridge the many ideological and policy issues that divided women activists at the time. According to historian Sara M. Evans, the deep differences among feminists cause some to "regularly challenge others' credentials as feminists . . . yet the energy of the storm that drives them all comes from their shared challenge to deeply rooted inequalities based on gender."[32] To borrow a broad definition of feminism from political scientist Barbara Arneil, feminism is

> the recognition that, virtually across time and place, men and women are unequal in the power they have, either in society or over their own lives, and the corollary belief that men and women should be equal; the belief that knowledge has been written about, by and for men and the corollary belief that all schools of knowledge must be reexamined and understood to reveal the extent to which they ignore or distort gender.[33]

The study of feminism also allows for a better understanding of various types of power and their influence on women's lives, as most feminists agree that men's power versus women's lack thereof determines their different experiences of society. Yet feminists "disagree on the extent, causes, and impact of these differences on the means and strategies for changing and improving the situation of women."[34] Despite the problems associated with categorizing various modes of feminist thought, the "old labels" are still useful insofar as they "signal to the broader public that feminism is not a monolithic ideology, that all feminists do not think alike, and that, like all other time-honored modes of thinking, feminist thought has a past as well as a present and a future."[35] Although the following discussion does not include every category of feminist thought, the most prominent feminist categories are highlighted. And it should be noted that there is sometimes a disconnect between the feminist theories developed and promoted by academic scholars and their practical applications by political leaders within the women's rights/ feminist movement.

Liberal Feminism

Liberal feminism is grounded in the quest for equal rights and fairness in society for women (for example, equal access to educational and employment opportunities, equal pay, and equal treatment in the eyes of the law). The first and second waves of the women's movement were greatly influenced by classical liberal thought, based on the writings of John Locke and John Stuart Mill among others, which emphasizes the value of individual rights, limited government, government by consent, competition, rational thought, and a system of government based on the right over the good (which means that procedural justice and fairness is more important than substantive justice). As a result, liberal feminism is based on the belief that "female subordination is rooted in a set of customary and legal constraints blocking women's entrance to and success in the so-called public world."[36]

Radical Feminism

Moving beyond the liberal tradition, radical feminism seeks to end political and legal patriarchy and to initiate a radical overhaul of social and cultural institutions (like the family and the church). Radical feminists believe that sexism must be eradicated and that sex-gender roles that cause women's oppression within society must be changed. Various subgroups of radical feminists exist, but the two main groups include radical-libertarian and radical-cultural feminists. Radical-libertarian feminists believe that "the very concept of femininity as well as women's reproductive and sexual roles and responsibilities often serve to limit women's development as full human persons."[37] Radical-cultural feminists believe that the differences between men and women serve as barriers that "empower men and disempower women" but also that being feminine is better than being masculine. Therefore, they argue, women should not try to be more like men since there are fundamental personality differences between men and women, and that women's characteristics are special and should be celebrated.[38] In general, radical feminists support the notion that there are biological differences between men and women and attempt to draw lines between biologically determined behavior and culturally determined behavior in order to free both men and women as much as possible from their narrow gender roles within society.

Marxist-socialist Feminism

Another long-standing school of feminist thought is Marxist-socialist feminism. Relying on the basic premise of socialism found in the nineteenth-century writings of Karl Marx, this group of feminists believes that capitalism and patriarchy work together to oppress women within society. As a result, political, social, and economic structures need reform, and wealth must be redistributed to promote equality. There is a gendered division of labor within society, and women's work is always undervalued or devalued. Under the Marxist view of capitalism, those controlling the means of production control workers; the few control the many through private business ownership. To break the cycle of a society based on economic classes, a socialist system (characterized by government control and ownership) must be created so that the means of production are owned by all within society and not just a powerful few. Marxist-socialist feminists believe that this type of reform will give women greater power and equality within the public sphere.

Black, Chicana, and Latina Feminism

In response to the narrow and exclusive form feminism took during the second wave of the women's rights movement, women of color began to promote a more humanist view of feminism based on the intersection of race, class, and gender. As a result, black feminism, Chicana feminism, and Latina feminism emerged and brought a unique contribution to feminist thought, since these women have experienced two forms of discrimination within society based on their sex and racial/ethnic background. Their respective views provide a better balance to the feminist theories supported by white women. The black feminist movement grew out of, and in response to, the black liberation movement and the women's movement during the 1960s as many black women felt they were being racially oppressed in the white-dominated women's movement and sexually oppressed by the male leadership in the black liberation movement. Black feminists wanted to develop a theory that would adequately address the ways in which race, gender, and class were interconnected and to take action to stop racist, sexist, and classist discrimination.[39]

The Chicana feminist movement also emerged during the 1960s as Chicana feminists assessed both their life circumstances and their participation in the larger Chicano social protest movement. The policy concerns Chicanas considered most pressing included welfare rights, reproductive rights, health care, poverty, immigration, and education.[40] The political mobilization of Latina feminists has also been shaped by similar concerns about employment, poverty, education, health, child care, reproductive rights, and political empowerment within their communities. The term *Latina* is often broadly used to include women of different ethnic backgrounds, including Mexican American, Cuban American, Puerto Rican American, Central American, and Latin American. However, *Latina/Latino* may also be used inclusively to refer to any person of Latin American ancestry residing in the United States, connoting identification with Indo-American heritage rather than Spanish European heritage. Latina feminists share a strong allegiance with other feminists of color in the United States.

Other Feminisms

Various other views of feminist thought have emerged within academic and political circles in the years since the second wave of the women's movement. Postmodern feminists reject classical liberal labels and believe that social, cultural, and political categories are socially constructed. Thus, postmodern feminists want to deconstruct the notion of truth as we know it and offer a critique of liberalism and the systems and categories that privilege men over women. This view presents both a dichotomy and a dilemma for feminists, since the postmodern view suggests that there is no inherent legitimacy to the current system. Whereas feminists have succeeded by labeling women as privileged groups (through legislation and court cases), postmodern feminists claim that identifying women as a separate group within society is a worthless exercise.

Multicultural/global feminists point out that all women are

not the same; that cultural, racial, and ethnic differences among women should be acknowledged; and that one class of privileged, mostly white, women cannot speak for all women on the issue of equality and rights. Transnational/third-world feminism focuses on globalization, the political economics of power, and the role of the state in shaping the day-to-day lives of women around the world; the state is viewed as a dominant power over women due to its "gendered, patriarchal, racialized, and (hetero)sexualized" practices.[41] Psychoanalytic feminism deals with the way society constructs masculine and feminine behavior, and argues that femininity is rooted in social expectations of gendered behavior from early childhood that separate males from females, thus taking root in women's psyches. As a result, a more humanist or androgynous approach is necessary to move away from the emphasis on male and female traits. Gender feminism is similar in positing that there is a psychological as well as a biological explanation for the differences between masculine and feminine traits. Finally, ecofeminism argues that women and nature are connected and that both are harmed by patriarchy's hierarchical system of oppression. This theory rests on the basic principle that patriarchal philosophies are harmful to women, children, and other living things. Parallels are drawn between society's treatment of the environment, animals, and resources and its treatment of women.

■ Conclusion

The history of the women's movement, women's rights, and feminisms in the United States is a diverse and complex one, revealing how women have banded together and also clashed with each other in an attempt to define their preferred place in US society. The system of public and private spheres that defined a woman's role in society has long served as the catalyst for numerous generations of women fighting for political and legal equality. No one movement, cause, or theory can encapsulate the needs of all women, yet significant progress has been made since the nineteenth century in bringing about political and legal reforms in regard to women's equality. Prominent women leaders such as Elizabeth Cady Stanton, Susan B. Anthony, Carrie Chapman Catt, Betty Friedan, Gloria Steinem, Rebecca Walker, and countless others have dedicated much of their lives to fighting for the right for women to enter the public realm at various points in our nation's history. Although many barriers for women entering public life have been torn down, many challenges lie ahead. As we discuss in the following chapters, women in today's political environment still face many obstacles in terms of entering the political arena, yet the legacy of the modern women's movement has provided many more opportunities for them than they have had in any prior generation.

■ Study/Discussion Questions

1. Why was the first wave of the women's movement so closely tied to both the temperance and abolitionist movements of the nineteenth century?

2. Discuss the impact that Elizabeth Cady Stanton and Susan B. Anthony's leadership had on the early women's rights movement.

3. Why did it take nearly seventy-five years after the Seneca Falls Convention for women to earn the right to vote in the United States?

4. What is meant by the separation of the public and private spheres, and why did feminists view this system as oppressive to women?

5. What influence did Betty Friedan's *The Feminine Mystique* have on the second wave of the women's movement?

6. How does the third wave differ from the second wave of the women's movement?

7. How do liberal and radical feminists differ? What impact have women of color had on feminist views and debates?

■ Online Resources

Concerned Women for America. http://www.cwfa.org.
The Eagle Forum. http://www.eagleforum.org.
Feminist Majority Foundation. http://www.feminist.org.
Independent Women's Forum. http://www.iwf.org.
Ms. Magazine. http://www.msmagazine.com.

National Organization for Women. http://www.now.org.

The National Women's History Project. http://www.nwhp.org.

Places Where Women Made History. http://www.cr.nps.gov/nr/ travel/pwwmh/index.htm.

The Susan B. Anthony House. http://www.susanbanthonyhouse.org.

The Third Wave Foundation. http://www.thirdwavefoundation.org.

▧ Notes

1. Costain, "Paving the Way," 31.
2. Tindall and Shi, *America: A Narrative History*, 273.
3. Quoted in Levin, *Abigail Adams*, 82.
4. Epstein and Walker, *Constitutional Law for a Changing America*, 6.
5. Matthews, *Women's Struggle for Equality*, 5.
6. Morgan, "Introduction," xxxiii-xxxiv.
7. For example, see Jeydel, *Political Women*, 46–48.
8. Jeydel, *Political Women*, 80.
9. O'Brien, *Constitutional Law and Politics*, 1517.
10. See Mansbridge, *Why We Lost the ERA*, 1–7.
11. Harper, "Biography of Susan B. Anthony and Elizabeth Cady Stanton."
12. Miroff, *Icons of Democracy*, 125.
13. Ibid., 125–126.
14. Banner, "Elizabeth Cady Stanton," 742.
15. DuBois, "Susan B. Anthony," 38–39.
16. Evans, *Tidal Wave*, 18–19.
17. See Friedan, *It Changed My Life*.
18. Rosen, *The World Split Open*, 35.
19. *Ms. Magazine*, "HerStory."
20. Denes, "Feminism? It's Hardly Begun."
21. Henry, *Not My Mother's Sister*, 16–17.
22. Ibid.
23. See Evans, *Tidal Wave*, 230–232.
24. Henry, *Not My Mother's Sister*, 7.
25. For example, see Findlen, *Listen Up*, and Walker, *To Be Real*.
26. Michaels, "Stealth Feminists," 139.
27. Baumgardner and Richards, *Manifesta*, 17.
28. Costain, "Paving the Way," 36.
29. Rosenbloom, "Evolution of a Feminist Daughter."
30. Walker, "The Power of Palin."
31. Schreiber, *Righting Feminism*, 4.
32. Evans, *Tidal Wave*, 2–3.
33. Arneil, *Politics and Feminism*, 3–4.
34. Holvino, "Women and Power," 363–364.
35. Tong, *Feminist Thought*, 1.

36. Ibid., 2.
37. Ibid., 47.
38. Ibid., 47–49.
39. See Collins, *Black Feminist Thought*, 221–238.
40. See García, "The Development of Chicana Feminist Discourse, 1980."
41. Holvino, "Women and Power," 370–371.

3

Women as
Political Participants

I am a governor who happens to be a woman.
■ Former New Jersey governor Christine Todd Whitman,
in response to a reporter's question on
what it was like to be a woman governor

In the last few presidential elections, the most sought-after votes
for both Democratic and Republican candidates have been those
of women. Whether courting "soccer moms" (mostly college-educated, upper-middle-class, suburban, and predominantly white
women with school-age children) in 1996, "security moms"
(whose concerns about terrorism and national security compete
with more traditional women's issues such as education and health
care) in 2004, or offering the opportunity to vote for a woman
candidate in 2008 (Hillary Rodham Clinton's bid for the
Democratic nomination or Sarah Palin's pick as the Republican
vice presidential nominee in 2008), presidential contenders and
their strategic advisers have targeted women as the key to winning
a presidential election. In 2008, women voters played a significant
role in Barack Obama's election despite both his hard-fought contest with Clinton in the primaries and Palin's presence on the
Republican ticket in the general election. Earlier, in 2004, undecided women voters were targeted in swing states by the campaigns of both incumbent Republican George W. Bush and
Democrat John Kerry, if for no other reason than the fact that
voter turnout had been higher among women than among men in
every presidential election since 1980. In both 2004 and 2008, sig-

nificant efforts were made by both parties to increase the number
of women who registered and voted, especially among the large
number of undecided women voters late in the presidential contest. And in both campaigns, a seven-point gender gap—that is,
the difference in the proportion of women and men voting for a
particular candidate—showed that women favored the
Democratic candidate. In recent years, Democrats have maintained an advantage with women voters, while Republicans have
continued their efforts to close the gap.[1]

Regardless of gender, voter turnout remains an issue in the
United States, which ranks lower than many other industrialized
democracies in this regard (including Belgium, Italy, France,
Denmark, Austria, Germany, Great Britain, Canada, and Japan).
The US government is based on democratic principles with a
strong emphasis on citizen participation. It is this emphasis that
distinguishes a democratic society from other types of government where citizens are not involved in the election of officials or
the policymaking process. In the United States, it means that sov-
ereignty lies with the people; for self-government to work, people
have a right and an obligation to participate in government. But
people must be given meaningful opportunities to participate, and
the level of that participation is a measure of how fully democratic
the society is. Women did not have the right to participate in the
political process as voters until 1920, with the passage of the
Nineteenth Amendment, but even then, not all women rushed to
the ballot box to cast their vote in elections, and public opinion
still did not favor women's full participation in public life. Due to
factors such as social, cultural, and legal barriers, women throughout our nation's history have never been encouraged to become
full political participants. Even by the start of the twenty-first
century, women were still contending with negative stereotypes
that served as barriers to political participation. This chapter considers women as political participants—voters, members of political parties and interest groups, and members of the news media. It
is important to learn how women vote and why and to consider
the significance of the gender gap in US politics. We must also ask
how political parties and interest groups represent women's issues
and court support from women. The socialization process, including the role of the news media, is also important to this discussion, revealing how women think about politics in general—about

their role as voters, about policy issues relevant to them, and about how they view women candidates as potential political leaders.

■ Women and Political Socialization

How women define themselves as political participants depends on the process of *political socialization*, or the ways in which people acquire their political opinions, beliefs, and values. There are several agents of socialization, and many of them overlap. Early in life, these agents include family members and school. Parents can be very influential on a child's early beliefs, and many adults end up having the same political party affiliation and views on certain policies as their parents. What children learn in school, especially at the primary level, has been shown to be an idealized and heroic version of US history and politics. Studies have also shown that college-educated adults tend to show stronger support for individual rights and for political involvement and awareness than their less-educated counterparts. Peer groups can also influence how their members think about political issues, since these groups tend to have similar political views and being a member of the group can reinforce what a person already believes. Religious groups and churches are also important agents of political socialization, as are political leaders and political institutions. One of the more powerful influences on the political socialization process is the mass media, which can provide strong images and can perpetuate stereotypical views of groups, including women, in society. Even more directly related to the political process is the impact of the news media, which can affect one's political views by the way it frames or sets the agenda for the news, deciding which stories are covered and which are not. The news media may not be able to tell us what to think, but it can tell us what to think about.

As we discussed in Chapter 2, the split between the public and private spheres has served as a formidable barrier for women attempting to enter politics in the United States, fostering negative attitudes about women's political participation. From the time women first received the right to vote in 1920, that negative cultural attitude about women's political participation has represented an informal barrier to those seeking public office. As the twentieth century wore on, public opinion polls showed a slow decrease in the percentage of Americans who believed that women did not belong as participants in the political process or office-holders. Cultural attitudes began to change more rapidly by the start of the modern women's movement in the 1960s, and women began having more success in political campaigns. Yet the political socialization process continues to plague women's efforts in the political arena, as girls are still not socialized to take an active role in politics, with several studies showing that girls tend to show less interest in and have less knowledge of politics than boys. However, women most likely to run for office have parents who vote in every election and who encouraged their daughters to be politically active.[2]

Political attitudes toward women in politics have changed as more women have been elected to office, moving away from the outdated belief that women do not belong in public life. According to political scientist Kathleen Dolan,

> a public that believes that a woman's place is in the home is unlikely to vote for any woman candidates with the courage to run. However, if voters feel that women have an equal role to play in political life, they can use these attitudes as a baseline against which they can evaluate individual women candidates and decide if they are worthy of support. . . . [T]he increased success of women candidates during the past 30 years or so has been mirrored by a gradual shifting in attitudes about women's place in political life.[3]

How women view other women as potential political candidates may also be driven by traditional social norms about "appropriate" female behavior. According to political scientist Ruth B. Mandel, women may face a cultural barrier to winning elected office due to the "incongruence between their sex-role socialization and the characteristics and behavior necessary to wage a successful campaign. Although socialized to exhibit values and behaviors considered appropriate for females, in running for office women enter into a sphere of life dominated by masculine values and behavior patterns."[4] As more women win campaigns and hold political office, the view of women as effective political leaders will more than likely continue to shift public attitudes about the efficacy of women in public life.

■ **Women and the Mass Media**

As one of the most important agents of political socialization, the mass media and more specifically the news media plays an important role in how women are viewed as current and/or potential political leaders. Theories abound as to how people receive information through the mass media. Some scholars suggest that the media has a powerful impact on society and that people may actually need to be protected from its effects. For example, viewers can be led to believe that reality mirrors the images in the mass media, and thus women and minorities can develop poor self-esteem due to negative stereotyping by media sources. A contrasting theory, known as the minimal effects approach, suggests that the mass media have a weak impact on society, since people only expose themselves to media content that goes along with their current views or perceptions. Other theories, like the uses and gratifications approach or the media systems dependency approach, suggest that people use the media toward a specific end, whether it is to be informed, entertained, or to escape from their daily routines (some people even become dependent on this use).[5]

And what images of women are being portrayed in the mass media? Throughout the 1970s, movies and television were male dominated. Women were relegated to traditional and stereotypical roles: wife, mother, homemaker, or, for those women not married, looking for love, romance, and marriage. Women were not portrayed as independent or career oriented; they appeared willing to give up their identities and ambitions for their husbands. Political news about women was mostly nonexistent and left to the women's pages of newspapers, including watershed moments in the women's movement such as the founding of the National Organization for Women in 1966. Even into the 1980s, according to political scientist David L. Paletz, the mass media took a rather narrow view of its portrayal of women: "Television's ideal feminine type was blonde, beautiful, and young; lesbians and African American women did not fit. Aging in women was depicted more negatively than in men, and older women were hard to find in television shows, other than on *Golden Girls*, where they behaved as if they were much younger."[6] The current representation of women is mixed—part traditional, part feminist. While some portrayals of women in films and on television starting in the 1990s finally began to reflect the diversity of women in US society in terms of race, ethnicity, socioeconomic status, education, occupation, marital status, and sexual preference, Paletz states that "ambivalent and contradictory images" of women remain as "women are told to assert themselves, pursue careers, enjoy their independence but also to defer to men and to work hard to look beautiful and thin. The media's overtly political content continues to represent and reinforce the 'political dominance of males over females.'"[7]

The mass media also perpetrates many negative stereotypes about women in US society. Stereotyping is the act of using a simplified mental image of an individual or group of people who share a certain characteristic or qualities; this allows people to quickly process information and categorize people based on what are often negative characteristics. In the political arena, voters also rely on sex stereotypes when forming impressions of political candidates, including some negative ones about women candidates' leadership abilities or qualifications for office. In certain situations, stereotyping of women candidates can be helpful. For example, if a particular elected position (like a mayor or state legislator) requires a great deal of effort in dealing with policies related to children or the elderly, then stereotyping a woman candidate as caring and compassionate could actually be beneficial. Yet that same stereotype could be seen as a negative quality for a woman running for the White House, since a president is expected to lead with tough and bold initiatives in the areas of defense and foreign policy.[8]

News coverage of women in general, but particularly of female professionals and athletes, often relies on stereotyping, and women are drastically underrepresented in coverage across all news outlets. Even with the steady increase of women in all professions, including politics, law, medicine, higher education, and the corporate world, most news coverage continues to rely on men, and not women, as experts in their respective fields. Women in the news are more likely to be featured in stories about accidents, natural disasters, or domestic violence than in stories about their professional abilities or expertise. This lack of gender balance in news coverage is an international problem, as a study by the Association of Women Journalists found in 2000. The organization studied news coverage of women and women's issues in seventy countries and found that (1) only 18 percent of stories quoted women and (2) the number of women-related stories came to just over 10 percent of total news coverage.[9] A lack of news coverage for women politicians can be particularly problematic if they are not portrayed as strong and capable leaders and as authoritative decisionmakers when it comes to public policy. This can be a difficult cycle to break, since women in Congress, for example, do not receive as much attention due to lack of seniority and leadership positions.[10] In addition, even as the media has a "romantic affair" with the topic of leadership, which figures in its recurring narrative about successes and failures around the globe, women leaders are frequently absent from its coverage. According to Karin Klenke, an expert on leadership studies, "Women leaders are either treated as a scarcity or are labeled ineffective because cultural stereotypes hold that they lack important leadership attributes."[11] Yet breaking the negative stereotypes and the portrayal of women as the political "other" in the news media is necessary to facilitate the continued progress of women in government.

Another important factor to consider is the number of women working in the news media industry, as well as the number of women in high-ranking positions within the industry. Even with the progress that women in general have made in a variety of professions in the past four decades, still only one-third of all journalists in the United States are women, with the highest percentages at weekly newspapers and news magazines and the lowest at wire services and in television.[12] Women in journalism had made great strides by the early 1990s, holding more positions within the industry than ever before, but very few held positions at the highest levels of decisionmaking. Women journalists have, in recent years, begun to broaden the definition of news to include more policy issues relevant to women, including women's health, child care, economic issues, and issues dealing with sexual discrimination and sexual harassment.[13] Yet the news media is still dominated by white men, both in the industry and in the coverage that is produced. In 2008, women held only 3 percent of the top leadership positions within the media, publishing, and entertainment fields. Only one-fourth of all television news directors are women, while no more than 15 percent of all radio programmers and managers are women. And as for newspapers, only 35 percent of supervisors are women, and only 39 percent of all reporters are women.[14] Therefore, the social and cultural norms that are reflected in a majority of news coverage do not represent the views of women or ethnic minorities, since "these internal constraints of media organizations and personnel, by necessity, dictate the ultimate news product."[15]

Then again, media outlets dedicated to women (as opposed to the mainstream news industry) have moved way beyond the women's pages of newspapers from the 1960s and 1970s to become a multibillion dollar industry, run in part by many powerful and influential women known as the "spin sisters." Women's magazines alone, like *Glamour, Cosmopolitan, Woman's Day, Good Housekeeping, Redbook,* and *Ladies Home Journal,* just to name a few, are part of a US\$7 billion-a-year industry. Network television targets much of its news programming in the morning (like NBC's *The Today Show* and ABC's *Good Morning America*) and in prime time (NBC's *Dateline,* ABC's *Primetime* and *20/20,* and CBS's *48 Hours*) at women viewers, with an emphasis on emotional human interest stories or the latest consumer news about health risks. In addition, ABC's *The View,* a roundtable talk show hosted by Barbara Walters, Whoopi Goldberg, Joy Behar, Sherry Shepherd, and Elizabeth Hasselbeck, remains one of the top-rated morning television programs. Cable television advertisers have also discovered the power of women as a demographic group, considering them much more influential in purchasing decisions than men and thus courting them on networks such as *Lifetime,* whose motto is "Television for women," and *Oxygen,* whose stated mission is to bring women "the edgiest, most innovative entertainment on television." The afternoon talk show circuit is still dominated by Oprah Winfrey, one of the wealthiest and most powerful women in the United States, along with other women hosts, including Ellen DeGeneres and Tyra Banks, as well as former hosts with high ratings, including Rosie O'Donnell. And while this part of the media industry may be run by the spin sisters, the message to women readers and viewers may not always be positive. According to Myrna Blyth, a former spin sister and editor of a major women's magazine, the message in women's media is not only potentially negative and misleading but comes with a liberal bias:

> I know from long experience that media for women tells you endlessly about the stress in your life, about the way you should look, about what should make you feel sorry for yourself, or very, very fearful about your health and the environment. In much the same way you are given a one-sided message about politics, too, by always being told more government is the best

Katherine Graham: The Power Behind the Front Page

Both Katherine Graham (1917–2001) and her newspaper, the *Washington Post*, left an indelible mark on both politics and the news media industry in America. Graham's father, Eugene Meyer, had purchased the *Post* in 1933 and served as its publisher until his death in 1946. Graham's husband, Philip Graham, then took over as publisher and was responsible for purchasing *Newsweek* magazine as part of the Washington Post Company. Philip Graham committed suicide in 1963, leaving his wife Katherine, a homemaker and mother of four, with control of the company. From 1969 until 1979, she served as publisher of the newspaper and then as board chairman and chief executive officer of the company from 1973 until 1991, remaining chairman of the executive committee until her death.

Due to the influence of the *Post* as one of the leading news sources among political elites not only within Washington but also throughout the nation and world, Graham was considered one of the most powerful women in America.[16] Under her leadership as publisher and through the investigative work of reporters Carl Bernstein and Bob Woodward, the *Post* led the news industry with its exposure of the Watergate scandal and played a prominent role in the resignation of President Richard Nixon in 1974 (Woodward and Bernstein won the Pulitzer Prize for reporting). In 1971, she allowed the *Post* (at the same time as the *New York Times*) to print excerpts from the top-secret Pentagon Papers, which detailed the history and decisionmaking process of US military involvement in Vietnam. This was done against the advice of the newspaper's attorneys and against government directives. In the famous *Pentagon Papers* case (*US v. New York Times*) that came before the US Supreme Court in the summer of 1971, the Nixon administration attempted unsuccessfully to stop the publication of the documents in both the *Post* and the *Times* by citing concerns for national security. A majority of the justices disagreed and claimed that the federal government could not impose prior restraint on the nation's leading newspapers to stop publication of the stories. It was during this time period that the *Post* developed its strong reputation within the news industry for its hard-hitting investigations and solidified its position as a leader among nationally read newspapers.

In 1997, Graham published her memoirs, *Personal History*. The autobiography won the Pulitzer Prize in 1998 and was praised for its honest portrayal of her husband's manic depression, which led to his suicide. She was also honest about her trepidation in taking over the newspaper after her husband's death: "I had very little idea of what I was supposed to be doing, so I set out to learn. What I essentially did was to put one foot in front of the other, shut my eyes, and step off the edge."[17] As a tribute, Graham's Washington funeral was broadcast live on major media outlets across the country and brought together political and media elites to extol "her character, skill, and contributions" to the worlds of both journalism and politics.[18]

solution to fix many of the problems in your life. That's a philo-
sophically loaded message that is the culmination of all the other
stories you are told about how tough life is for women, even
middle-class women.[19]

■ Women as Voters

Between 1920, when women first gained the right to vote, and
1980, women voted at lower rates than men. There are several
explanations for this trend, including (1) a backlash from the antisuffrage movement in the early part of the century that left many
women uninclined to vote and (2) a lack of positive political
socialization for young girls and women to encourage them to
become active political participants well into the 1980s. However,
that trend has reversed itself; in every presidential election since
1980, women have voted at a higher rate than men. For example,
roughly 7.8 million more women than men voted in 2000, a statis-
tic that helps to explain the attention that political parties and
presidential candidates have paid to the women's vote in recent
campaigns. In 2004, a nonpartisan effort called Women's Voices,
Women's Vote targeted unmarried women, as did respective partisan efforts by the Bush campaign (W Stands for Women) and
Kerry campaign (Women for Kerry).[20] Although the most prominent issues during the campaign were terrorism, national security,
and the war in Iraq, more subtle messages were being promoted
by both candidates to target women voters, particularly those who
were presumably undecided until the last few days of the campaign. Media strategies even included several appearances by both
candidates and their surrogates (that is, their spouses, children,
and respective running mates and *their* spouses and children) on
popular daytime television shows with traditionally high female
viewership like *The View*, *Live with Regis and Kelly*, and *Dr. Phil*
(George W. and Laura Bush and John and Teresa Heinz Kerry
each made appearances on the latter show to talk about their
respective marriages).[21] In 2008, with domestic issues and the
economy dominating the presidential campaign, similar tactics to
court women voters emerged. Both Barack Obama and John
McCain, as well as their spouses, made high-profile appearances
on *The View* and *Ellen*. Obama also had the early endorsement of
Oprah Winfrey, the first endorsement that she ever gave a presi-

dential candidate, and McCain selected Sarah Palin as his running mate in an attempt to appeal to women voters, particularly former supporters of Hillary Rodham Clinton in the Democratic primary.

Since 1980, much scholarly and news media attention has been paid to the issue of a gender gap in US elections, which explains the differences between men and women in their party identification and voting choice. In general, election results suggest that women are more likely to identify with and vote for the Democratic Party and its candidates, whereas men are more likely to support the Republican Party and its candidates. Between 1980 and 1992, the gap was between 4 and 8 percent, rising to 11 percent in both the 1996 and 2000 presidential campaigns. Election results have shown that the gender gap is larger among white than nonwhite voters. It is also larger among voters at higher socioeconomic levels, voters with more formal education, unmarried voters, and voters without children.[22] By the 2004 and 2008 presidential elections, the gender gap had been reduced to only a seven-point difference, with 48 percent of women versus 55 percent of men voting to reelect George W. Bush in 2004, and 56 percent of women versus 49 percent of men voting to elect Barack Obama in 2008.

Although the gender gap has narrowed, it has been replaced by an even larger marriage gap. Polling throughout the fall 2004 campaign showed that although Kerry had a narrower lead among women voters than past Democratic candidates have enjoyed, his lead among single voters, particularly women, was anywhere between 20 and 30 percent. However, Bush had nearly as wide a lead among married voters, particularly women. The marriage gap had never been this wide, but pollsters attributed it to

> fundamentally different views of government and the direction of the country. Married people are more optimistic about the future and are more suspicious about government's ability to help them [which favors] Republicans. Unmarried people tend to view government as more able to provide solutions to problems and are more pessimistic about the future of the country [which favors] Democrats.[23]

The marriage gap continued to play a major role in the 2008 presidential campaign, particularly for women voters. An overwhelming majority—70 percent—of unmarried women voters supported

Obama, with only 29 percent supporting McCain; in 2004, 62 percent of unmarried women had voted for Kerry, whereas 37 percent had voted for Bush. Among married women, 50 percent voted for McCain while 47 percent voted for Obama (in 2004, 55 percent had voted for Bush, 44 percent for Kerry).[24]

The first use of the term *gender gap* is credited to Eleanor Smeal, who talked about the trend while president of the National Organization for Women in 1981. US journalists quickly picked up on the phrase and popularized it as convenient shorthand to refer to gender differences in support for Democrats and Republicans. According to political scientist Pippa Norris, the role of gender in US politics helped to create an electoral realignment in 1980, revealing "a seismic shift in voting choice and party identification, which has subsequently been consolidated over successive elections. This development has had important consequences for party competition, for the recruitment of women candidates for elected office, and for the salience of gendered issues on the American policy agenda."[25] However, Norris warns that the many aspects of the gender gap phenomenon require further study to better understand the complexities of gender and its impact on voting behavior:

> Gender realignment has now become an established part of American elections, taken for granted by commentators, journalists, and politicians. It provides a useful frame or "peg" on which to hang different stories about the election. Nevertheless, we should not be seduced by the conventional wisdom as many assumptions surrounding this phenomenon remain underexplained.[26]

One of the most important issues to point out about the gender gap is that it does not necessarily provide an advantage to one particular party (usually assumed to be the Democratic Party) or a particular candidate. It simply means that men and women vote differently.[27] It is also important to remember that women do not constitute a monolithic voting bloc. As Richard A. Seltzer and his colleagues have pointed out in their study of women candidates, women as voters represent a "diverse and heterogeneous group of voters, not the special interest group that the term *the women's vote* implies. There are conservative and liberal women, antichoice and prochoice, women who oppose affirmative action and those who support it. The answer to the question 'What do women want?' depends on which women you ask."[28] Women candidates also do not automatically attract or win the support of women voters. Although women do tend to support women candidates by a slight advantage in most elections, partisanship among voters is still a better predictor of the outcome of a race in which a woman candidate is on the ballot than is the sex of the voter. For example, for all of the excitement that her candidacy generated among conservative voters in 2008, Sarah Palin failed to garner the support of independent or crossover Democratic voters (which the McCain campaign counted on by selecting her in an attempt to appeal to former Clinton supporters), due to many of her socially conservative views. The gender gap can vary across states and can also vary depending on the key issues being discussed by the candidates (the gender gap can widen when, for instance, the media and the candidates themselves focus on gender-related issues).[29]

■ Women in Political Parties and Interest Groups

Although political parties and interest groups are not mentioned anywhere in the US Constitution, they nonetheless play a crucial role in the electoral and governing processes at both the federal and state levels. Among other framers, James Madison warned in *Federalist 10* against the dangers that factions (as we would now consider parties or interest groups) due to the potential for like-minded individuals to overtake the government based on popular passions for a particular issue. In spite of those warnings, and for better or worse, political parties developed and became a permanent part of our government, dictating how we select officeholders and how certain aspects of government, like Congress, are structured. Our Constitution also encourages the maintenance of a two-party, winner-take-all system through its use of single-member districts in which third-party candidates have little to no chance of gaining elected office. Interest groups also emerged throughout the nineteenth and twentieth centuries as an important way for the many diverse constituencies among the US electorate to band together and lobby government officials to either redress grievances or seek favorable policies and resources to benefit their particular policy agenda. While women have never formed a like-minded or monolithic group in terms of the fight for equal rights or other relevant policy issues, "many, if not most, of the efforts through which women have sought power in [US] history have involved organized, collective action."[30]

Women as political activists within the American political system is not a recent phenomenon, nor is it something that only occurred once women secured the right to vote in 1920. Whether they played a crucial role in the suffrage, abolition, or temperance movements or as political party volunteers or activists, women have participated in the political process on many levels since the mid-nineteenth century. And because political parties play such a large role in our electoral and governing process, it is important to understand how women have historically fit into the overall party structure. By the start of the twentieth century, the three types of female political activists were feminists, reformers, and party women. Feminists were those women working solely for suffrage; reformers represented a variety of interests; party women belonged in both camps. According to Jo Freeman (who has written extensively on the history of women within political parties), after 1920, feminists and reformers struggled to survive, whereas party women

> undertook the task of mobilizing women to vote. It was party women who had the resources, and the reason, to do this. And it was the ranks of party women who were augmented by the increased political interest in politics by women who had not been involved in anything political prior to 1920. . . . the political parties recruited, organized, absorbed, and co-opted large numbers of politically inclined women.[31]

From 1920 to the mid-1960s, women's roles within political parties consisted of some work on party committees and in segregated political clubs. Women did much work with few rewards, garnering the image of "worker bees" within the party yet lacking real influence on policy issues. However, with the onset of the second wave of the women's movement in the late 1960s, this type of work within the parties laid the essential groundwork for women to play a larger role in terms of party platforms and policy agendas. As Freeman concludes, the presence of women in political parties throughout the twentieth century helped to civilize politics, replacing the male-dominated backroom approach to decisionmaking with one more accessible to women and "accelerat[ing] the shift in campaign techniques from emotional appeals to an emphasis on facts."[32]

In addition to how women have changed the internal structure within parties, the parties themselves have shaped policy debates to court women voters. It is therefore important to understand how (1) political parties have responded to the changes in voters' attitudes about women's ever-expanding public role in recent decades, and (2) Democrats and Republicans have differed on various women's issues. Although it is the Democratic Party that supported the causes of the second wave of the women's movement (most prominently the ERA, reproductive and abortion rights, and other legal issues such as pay equity and sexual harassment) and that supports third-wave feminist issues, it is actually the Republican Party that has a longer history of support for the ERA and other women's issues, dating back to the first half of the twentieth century. The Republican Party platform consistently included the ERA from 1940 until it was dropped in 1980 with the party's nomination of Ronald Reagan (due to the conservative shift within the National Republican Party since then, the ERA has not returned to the platform). In contrast, Democrats were slow to publicly support the ERA. It did not receive consistent support in the party's platform, nor did all Democratic presidents embrace the idea. For example, although Democrat John F. Kennedy took several steps to address the issues presented to him by the President's Commission on the Status of Women, a committee that he established in 1961, his administration did not publicly support the ERA. By contrast, Republican Richard Nixon, whose years in the White House (1969–1974) corresponded with rapid growth in the women's movement across the nation, went on record in support of the ERA as a presidential candidate in 1968. The next two presidents, Republican Gerald Ford (1974–1977) and Democrat Jimmy Carter (1977–1981), would also publicly support and campaign for passage of the ERA.[33]

Since the 1980 election and the emergence of the gender gap, the two parties differ in terms of how they represent women's issues, although the differences are often not as stark as most assume. As political scientist Kira Sanbonmatsu points out, the single issue of abortion is often mistakenly used as the standard-bearer of how parties differ on women's issues. Sanbonmatsu argues that Democrats and Republicans have both presented a more moderate stance on women's issues other than abortion in recent years. Both parties continue to address such so-called women's issues as equality, workforce participation, child rearing, and family responsibilities but in so doing they "combine a mix of traditional and nontraditional views about the role of women"; Democrats may be more attentive to women's issues than Republicans, yet "party leaders do not usually want elections to turn on gender debates."[34] The public has also remained "ambivalent about the changing role of women" despite the often intense and heated rhetoric on gender-related issues among both interest group and party elites.[35] Aside from that of abortion, party platforms rarely offer conflicting policy stances on women's issues. In recent presidential elections, both parties have agreed on the importance of issues like enforcing sex discrimination laws, improving child care options, more funding for women's health issues, and strengthening the traditional family. There is, in Sanbonmatsu's words, "little discussion of women in politics, but the platforms are similar to the extent they discuss them" at all.[36] The party leadership also remains male dominated; even if there is "parity in party organizational membership, party leadership for women remains rare."[37]

As we have already discussed, women have long been participants in activist causes and social movements. Interest groups have long served as the vehicles for various causes of concern to women, and, just as they did during the nineteenth century, they continue to provide women with leadership experience and opportunities within the political arena. Through lobbying and public education efforts, women's interest groups now represent a wide array of issues and ideological stances, and their political action committees (PACs), which provide monetary support for candidates, can play an influential role in election outcomes. And unlike political parties, which must represent numerous issues and constituencies under a wide umbrella, interest groups can focus on a much narrower range of policies and streamline their political and/or legislative efforts.

Older and more traditional women's interest groups include the League of Women Voters, the American Association of University Women, and Business and Professional Women. The League of Women Voters, founded in 1920 by suffragist leader

Carrie Chapman Catt, is a nonpartisan group dedicated to educating the public on political issues and candidates and to lobbying for government and social reform legislation. Throughout its history, the League of Women Voters has been "an activist, grassroots organization whose leaders believe that citizens should play a critical role in advocacy." Both campaign finance and election reform have been among its policy priorities.[38] The American Association of University Women, founded in 1881, promotes educational equity for women and girls; its foundation funds relevant research and provides a legal advocacy fund for women who have experienced sexual discrimination in higher education. Similarly, Business and Professional Women, founded in 1919, promotes equity for women in the workplace through advocacy and education, including professional development programs, networking opportunities, and scholarship funds.

Newer women's interest groups emerged in the context of protest politics in the second wave of the women's movement. Most prominent is the National Organization for Women, founded in 1966; the Women's Equity Action League, founded in 1968; and the National Women's Political Caucus, founded in 1971. These organizations (with the exception of the Action League, which disbanded in 1989) remain committed to pursuing a feminist agenda within US politics, advocating equity, reproductive rights, and a variety of other public policies related to health care, welfare, child care, and the environment, just to name a few. Other groups also emerged as an alternative for women who do not support the feminist agenda, such as the Eagle Forum (founded in 1972), Concerned Women for America (founded in 1979), and the Independent Women's Forum (founded in 1992).

Women's PACs, which are founded by women to raise money primarily or exclusively for female candidates, have experienced tremendous growth since the 1970s. They have also made important financial contributions to women candidates in addition to providing training, consultation, and workers in support of women candidates. These fund-raising groups, "like female activists and candidates . . . extend across the partisan and ideological spectrum."[39] Four of the most prominent women's PACs include EMILY's List (which stands for Early Money Is Like Yeast, meaning "it makes the dough rise" by providing early seed money for campaigns), which supports prochoice Democratic

Kim Gandy: Leading NOW into the Twenty-first Century

Since its founding in 1966, the National Organization for Women (NOW) has witnessed many changes on the US political landscape. The women's movement and feminism have experienced many public highs and lows since the 1960s, but NOW remains the largest feminist organization in the United States, with more than 500,000 members and 550 chapters nationwide. The organization counts among its former presidents feminist icons Betty Freidan, Eleanor Smeal, Molly Yard, and Patricia Ireland. More recently, Kim Gandy, who served as president from 2001–2009, took over the top post following Patricia Ireland's ten-year tenure. Gandy, an attorney and former assistant district attorney in New Orleans, is a longtime activist who has served in leadership positions for NOW at the local, state, and national levels since 1973, spending three years as the president of the Louisiana chapter. In 1991, she directed the WomenElect 2000 Project, a grassroots campaign in Louisiana whose organizing and recruiting efforts over the course of nine months increased voter turnout among women, tripled the number of women in the state legislature, and, led to the election of the first woman lieutenant governor in Louisiana.[40]

When first elected president of NOW, Gandy faced the challenge of leading her organization during a time when the Republican Party, in control of both the White House and Congress, was pursuing a social conservative agenda that opposed almost every political issue that NOW supports. In addition to promoting the traditional policy issues on NOW's agenda, like reproductive rights and equality for women in the workplace, Gandy led the effort to publicly fight a variety of issues that the Bush administration pursued, including the privatization of Social Security, Medicare reform, and a constitutional amendment banning same-sex marriages. In addition, NOW pursued an aggressive strategy in its attempt to block the nomination of various conservative federal judges by the Bush administration.

However, on the Democratic side of politics, support from NOW is not always automatic. In 2004, while Gandy and NOW/PAC endorsed Democrat John Kerry for president in 2004, he was not the organization's first choice. In August 2003, NOW/PAC, along with the National Women's Political Caucus, endorsed the candidacy of former US Senator and Ambassador

continues

Kim Gandy *continued*

Carol Moseley Braun for the Democratic presidential nomination. According to a NOW press release, to receive such an endorsement, a candidate "must demonstrate an uncompromising commitment to the entire range of women's rights issues. . . . After considering the positions and past records of all the candidates lined up to challenge George W. Bush, one candidate stood above the rest. . . . Moseley Braun's candidacy is a prime example of what feminists strive for—women moving up through all levels of political office. We are proud to have this strong and accomplished woman running for the highest office in the land—and serving as an inspiration to women and girls of all ages who believe that a woman truly can become president of the United States."[41] A *New York Times* editorial, however, called the endorsement "silly" and Moseley Braun's campaign nothing more than a "vanity affair."[42] Taking issue with the opinion of one of the nation's most influential newspapers, Gandy responded: "One of the reasons women had to struggle so long to win the vote—and why we continue to fight for full equality—is the trivializing of women and our concerns. It smacks of sexism when the endorsement of two major women's organizations is demeaned as 'silly.' And it smacks of more than that when a qualified African American woman is disparaged not for her experience or platform but for her presumed 'vanity.'. . . Moseley Braun, a forceful ally with a strong record, is getting women's issues onto the table and into the political debate—and she deserves our support. We've never made endorsements to impress the media or the pundits, and we're not going to start now. That would be silly."[43] In 2008, NOW initially endorsed Hillary Rodham Clinton in the Democratic primaries, yet individual chapters differed from the national organization by supporting Barack Obama. Despite the disappointment among many NOW members that Clinton failed in her bid to get the Democratic nomination, Gandy and NOW announced their support of Obama during the general election: "NOW supported Sen. Hillary Clinton in the primary, and now we join with her in saying 'NO—No Way, No How, No McCain!' And we proudly stand arm-in-arm with her in putting our hopes and our dreams, our hard work and our hard-earned money, behind the next President of the United States—Barack Obama, and his running mate, longtime friend and ally of women, Sen. Joe Biden."[44]

female candidates; The WISH (Women in the Senate and House) List, which supports prochoice Republican female candidates; the Women's Campaign Fund, a nonpartisan group that supports pro-choice female candidates; and The Susan B. Anthony List, which supports prolife female candidates (and claims that the group's namesake was opposed to legalized abortion). Women's PACs and their success are both "a product of and reaction to" the second wave of the women's rights movement. Notable diversity among these groups is attributed, in part, to the polarization on gender-related issues and reproductive rights between the Democratic and Republican parties. Yet as "divided as they are on fundamental questions about the role of government, [women's PACs] collectively have enhanced the representation of women in elective office . . . [and] have altered the government agenda."[45]

■ Conclusion

As this chapter demonstrates, women have experienced a varied and diverse history in regard to their roles as participants in the US political process. Scholars may continue to debate the electoral significance of the gender gap in voting patterns, but women continue to vote at a higher rate than men and still make up more than half of the voting population. Therefore, whether liberal or conservative or somewhere in between, whether Democrat or Republican or independent, women voters play a significant role in the development of campaign strategies and policy agendas at all levels of government. Although they still have a long way to go to achieve more leadership positions within political parties, reaching out to women voters across the ideological spectrum remains a top priority for both Democratic and Republican candidates. Gender issues have become part of the political branding process, since "at the end of the twentieth century the gender gap in party identification was no longer just a by-product of differences in ideology and socioeconomic status between men and women. Each party seems to have developed a gender-specific appeal based on its image and policies."[46] To date, no major realignment has occurred based on women's issues, and those interest groups supportive of gender-specific issues do not dominate each party's agenda. However, increasing women's political participation in terms of voting, party and interest group leadership, and breaking down the negative stereotypes of women and particularly women candidates in the mass media will go a long way toward promoting women as political leaders at all levels of government.

■ Study/Discussion Questions

1. How does political socialization impact participation for women as voters and potential candidates? What are the contributing agents to political socialization?

2. What are some of the negative stereotypes of women portrayed in the mass media? How can stereotypes in news coverage of campaigns harm women candidates?

3. What is the gender gap between voters? How have voting patterns for men and women changed in recent decades?

4. How did women first enter party politics? How do Democrats and Republicans differ in their support of women's issues?

5. What role do women's interest groups and PACs play in electing women to public office?

■ Online Resources

American Association of University Women. http://www.aauw .org.
Business and Professional Women. http://www.bpwusa.org.
Democratic National Committee. http://www.democrats.org.
EMILY's List. http://www.emilyslist.org.
Independent Women's Forum. http://www.iwf.org.
League of Women Voters. http://www.lwv.org.
National Organization for Women. http://www.now.org.
National Women's Political Caucus. http://www.nwpc.org.
Republican National Committee. http://www.rnc.org.
The Susan B. Anthony List. http://www.sba-list.org.
The WISH List. http://www.thewishlist.org.
Women's Campaign Fund. http://www.wcfonline.org.
The Women's Media Center. http://www.womensmediacenter.
Women's Voices. Women Vote. http://www.wvwv.org.

■ **Notes**

1. Center for American Women and Politics, "The Gender Gap."
2. See McGlen et al., *Women, Politics, and American Society,* 68–72.
3. Dolan, *Voting for Women,* 42–43.
4. Mandel, "A Question About Women," 93–94.
5. Paletz, *The Media in American Politics,* 117–121.
6. Ibid., 135–137.
7. Ibid., 139.
8. See Kahn, *The Political Consequences of Being a Woman.*
9. Media Awareness Network, "Media Portrayals of Girls and Women."
10. Braden, *Women Politicians and the Media,* 18.
11. Klenke, *Women and Leadership,* 113.
12. Graber, *Mass Media and American Politics,* 87.
13. See Weaver, "Women as Journalists," and Mills, "What Difference Do Women Journalists Make?"
14. See Siegal, "Bias, Punditry, and the Press?"
15. Whitaker, "Women and Sex Stereotypes," 91.
16. Dye, *Who's Running America?* 104.
17. See Graham, *Personal History.*
18. Sapiro, *Women in American Society,* 250.
19. Blyth, *Spin Sisters,* 8.
20. Carroll, "Women Voters and the Gender Gap."
21. Sweet, "Courting the Ladies," 72.
22. Wayne, *The Road to the White House 2008,* 100–101.
23. Raasch, "Candidates Face Distinct Challenges in Courting Female Voters."
24. Women's Voices. Women Vote. "Unmarried Women Play Critical Role in Historic Election."
25. Norris, "The Gender Gap," 146–147.
26. Ibid., 166.
27. Seltzer, Newman, and Leighton, *Sex as a Political Variable,* 4.
28. Ibid., 6.
29. Cook, "Voter Reaction to Women Candidates," 69–71.
30. Baer, "Women, Women's Organizations, and Political Parties," 111.
31. Freeman, *A Room at a Time,* 4–5.
32. Ibid., 228–235.
33. See Martin, *The Presidency and Women.*
34. Sanbonmatsu, *Democrats/Republicans and the Politics of Women's Place,* 2.
35. Ibid., 91.
36. Ibid., 112.
37. Baer, "Women, Women's Organizations, and Political Parties," 134.
38. See the League of Women Voters home page at http://www.lwv.org.

39. Day and Hadley, *Women's PACs: Abortion and Elections*, 1.

40. National Organization for Women, "NOW Officers, Kim Gandy—President."

41. National Organization for Women, "NOW/PAC Endorses Carol Moseley Braun for President, Statement of NOW/PAC Chair Kim Gandy."

42. "NOW's Woman Problem," 10.

43. Gandy, "The *New York Times*' Woman Problem."

44. National Organization for Women, "National Organization for Women PAC Endorses Obama-Biden."

45. Ibid., 95.

46. Abramowitz, *Voice of the People*, 99.

4
Women as
Political Candidates

A new political consciousness was born that no longer asked "why" a woman candidate but "why not?" The real test of my candidacy will come when the next woman runs for national office.
■ Geraldine Ferraro, on her vice presidential candidacy in 1984

If women make up slightly more than half of the population in the United States, which translates into more than half of eligible voters, then why are women still so underrepresented in elected political office? Since finally gaining the right to vote in 1920, women have been making up for lost time in many areas of the political process. Yet despite the gains made since the 1970s, particularly in the area of political party and interest group participation (as discussed in Chapter 3), women candidates still face many barriers to achieving electoral success, including those imposed by the electoral process itself (such as incumbency and the reliance on funding of competitive campaigns); the stereotyping of women candidates; and the fact that women generally start their political careers later than men due, in part, to family demands. In addition to the structural impediments, one of the most important obstacles for women to overcome is simply making the decision to run for office; the general perception for many potential women candidates that they do not have a strong chance of winning, even if untrue, discourages women from tossing their hats in the ring and thus holding more seats in Congress, state legislatures, and even the White House.[1]

Yet a compelling argument can be made as to why more women should become public officeholders and why their leadership at the national, state, and local levels can make an important difference in terms of public policies. Women politicians have an ideological advantage: regardless of party affiliation, they are often in a better position to address certain societal needs relating to the overall welfare of citizens or to protest policies such as war. An increase in women's representation can also help to legitimize the political system and provide societal benefits as well with increased competition for public office.[2] In this chapter, we will consider women as political candidates and the unique challenges they face in running for office at all levels of government. Breaking into the system to become a political leader is not an easy task for women candidates, who face challenges within the party structure and in raising adequate funds to finance campaigns. Also, since the incumbency factor is so prevalent, giving members of Congress and other elected offices (such as legislatures in states without term limits) such a strong advantage, women and minority candidates often face an uphill battle toward parity in terms of representation. There also tends, as we have seen, to be a gender bias in news media coverage during campaigns, which can lead to negative stereotyping of women candidates. In this chapter, we look at how women are recruited to run for office, the institutional barriers to the electoral arena with which women candidates must contend, and the all-important image created for women candidates through the watchful eyes of the news media.

■ Recruiting Women Candidates

Do women receive adequate encouragement and support to run for political office? The initial decision to run is perhaps the most difficult for women to make for their own careers in the short run, yet the most crucial in the longer-term goal of placing more women in positions of political power. Although women candidates since the 1990s have shown that they can raise money competitively and win both congressional and statewide elections, there is still resistance to their candidacies. According to political scientist Ruth B. Mandel, many young women today have decided to shun the high-pressure, brutally competitive lifestyle that comes with many leadership opportunities, including those within the political arena. As a result, as the number of women in elected positions has leveled off since the early 1990s when the percentage of women holding congressional and state positions was increasing, many women are thinking twice before making the commitment to become a political candidate. As Mandel states,

> There is a continuing conundrum here. Nothing will change the picture of leadership and perhaps the practices of leadership unless women themselves choose to pursue leadership. In the United States, far and away, this matter of women's choices stands as the single greatest remaining challenge to achieving parity for women in leadership. . . . They confront more opportunities and options than ever before. Nonetheless, women must choose to walk the path.[3]

Anecdotal evidence about women's political experiences, whether in the recruitment or campaign phase, presents a mixed story. Whereas some women report facing hostility at trying to break into a traditionally male-dominated sphere like politics, others claim to have received tremendous enthusiasm and support from male political elites in their pursuit of public office.[4] Party leaders in the Democratic and Republican parties of the 1970s and 1980s were not overly committed to recruiting female candidates for Congress. Even when they did recruit women, they often failed to follow up by supporting their election to office once the campaign began. Patterns emerged to show that party leaders maintained contact with women candidates less frequently than with men and that women were often recruited to run as sacrificial lambs in districts where there was no hope of winning. The reluctance of both the Democratic and Republican parties to "approach women and to present them with the opportunity to run in races [with] at least some chance of general election victory [has been] an important feature of the political opportunity structure that inhibits substantial increases in the numerical representation of women among elective office holders."[5] By the early 1990s, however, analyses of congressional data show that women no longer ran disproportionately for unwinnable seats and were just as likely as men to receive encouragement regarding their candidacies from party leaders.[6]

Women seeking office in state legislatures have faced similar recruitment situations. The likelihood that a woman will run for a state legislative seat varies from state to state and ties in with other factors like incumbency, the number of eligible women in the recruitment pool, and the perceived viability of women candidates by party leaders. However, party recruitment can and does play a significant role in electing women legislators in some states. This process often begins at the local level, as local party leaders can provide important information to gatekeepers at the state level regarding which candidates may have the highest probability of winning an election. Therefore, evaluations by party leaders of potential candidates play a large role in determining who actually runs for office. According to political scientist Kira Sanbonmatsu, "Where the parties recruit candidates to run or formally or informally support candidates in the primary, party leaders can play a major role in shaping the social composition of the legislature. . . . In states with an organized recruitment process, whether that process yields women candidates very much depends on party leaders' perception of the quality and electability of women candidates and their personal knowledge of or access to names of potential women candidates."[7]

In terms of being eligible to run for political office, most women candidates have the necessary qualifications for the job—most are well educated and have professional or managerial careers (although few tend to be lawyers, perhaps due to the fact that women were in many respects barred from the legal profession until the 1970s). Most women candidates also have some party and organizational experience, although these types of qualifications in general appear to have little effect on election outcomes. Yet, with most political offices still dominated by men, the one qualification that a large number of women lack is prior office-holding experience. Particularly throughout the 1970s and 1980s, this seemed to represent an important barrier for women candidates. According to political scientist Susan Carroll, "It is not the case that those who are more qualified win while those who lack qualifications lose. The only variables that seemed to discriminate between winners and losers with any consistency were some measures of party activity and former office holding."[8] Prior political experience, particularly at the local level, can be a critical indicator of the number of women who will be seen as credible candidates for higher office. As Georgia Duerst-Lahti puts it, "Experience in one elected office is seen as providing credentials for other offices"; therefore, the pipeline or bottleneck by which women candidates must enter the political arena accounts for previous and current shortfalls.[9]

Political scientists are attempting to better understand the factors that may keep women from running for elected office. Incumbency, as we discuss even further in the next section, dominates much of the electoral process in Congress and state legislatures and serves as a structural barrier for all candidates, not just women. Yet there are still specific barriers to elected office that appear to be unique for potential women candidates. The primary reason for women's underrepresentation at all levels of government stems from the simple fact that women choose to run less frequently than men, even though, given similar levels of party and financial support, they are just as likely as men to win. The factors that seem to contribute to a woman's choice not to run include gender-specific political socialization (as discussed in Chapter 3), family responsibilities, lack of political confidence, and a lack of visible role models in politics.[10] Also, a critical gender difference exists in the candidate emergence phase due to a substantial winnowing process that yields a smaller ratio of women than men candidates. Women may be less likely to receive encouragement from party officials at this crucial phase, yet those who do choose to run tend to receive similar amounts of support from party leaders and other political groups. Women are also less likely to deem themselves qualified to run for political office, even when they have achieved great professional success. This suggests that "recruitment patterns—or lack thereof—appear to solidify women's self-perceptions."[11] In addition, women are often less interested in running for public office than men, and when women do run for office, they choose lower-level offices.[12]

■ Women Candidates and the Electoral Process

Regardless of the sex of the candidate, incumbency and money largely determine who actually gets elected in US political campaigns. The incumbency advantage, particularly in Congress, plays the largest role in determining election outcomes. Over time,

incumbent members of Congress are reelected in close to 95 percent of races. Sometimes that figure is even higher. In 2004, for
example, 98 percent of incumbents in the House of
Representatives and 96 percent of incumbents in the Senate were
reelected. There are many reasons for the incumbency advantage,
including name recognition, the ability to provide services for their
constituents (done with the help of congressional staffers) as well
as the ability to send free mail (known as franking) to voters within
their district, the ability to support legislation that their constituents also support, and the advantage over challengers in raising large amounts of money to fund their campaigns. In addition,
congressional races receive little news media coverage, which
leaves voters uninformed about the candidates and the relevant
issues; instead, they rely on name recognition and/or party loyalty
when casting a vote. As a result of all of these factors combined,
challengers tend to be weaker candidates—ironically enough, since
Americans tend to resoundingly dislike Congress as an institution,
yet they never seem to blame their individual representatives for
the problems of government waste and legislative gridlock.

Another, increasingly problematic, factor of the incumbency
advantage is the growing number of so-called safe seats. With the
help of redistricting, which occurs at the state level, political parties that hold the majority in state legislatures have been able to
create safe districts in which the candidates of opposing parties
have little or no chance of defeating incumbents. As a result, nearly one-fourth of all congressional seats in the most recent elections belong to incumbents who ran unopposed. This is particularly problematic for women and minority candidates trying to
break into the political arena, and it explains why both groups,
particularly women, tend to do better in open-seat elections
where there is no incumbent on the ballot. The incumbency
advantage, then, is the most valid explanation for the limited electoral success of women candidates. As Carroll points out,

> While incumbents tend to win elections at a much higher rate
> than nonincumbents, very few women candidates are incum-
> bents. Candidates who run against incumbents (and/or against
> candidates of the opposing party who have defeated incumbents
> in primaries) rarely win elections, and sizable numbers of
> women candidates run in races where they confront such situa-
> tions.[13]

Women have experienced a higher rate of electoral success in state legislatures due to a higher turnover rate for incumbents, since state legislators are more likely to return to their previous careers or run for higher office, thereby creating more open seats for challengers. (This is also due, in part, to the fact that some states, like Texas, have part-time legislators who earn low salaries and thus find it difficult to create a long-term career in the state capitol. Other states, like California, have full-time, well-paid state legislators, but their time in office is governed by mandatory term limits.)

One study of women candidates showed that women's success rates were identical to men's when comparing incumbent women and men, when comparing women and men running for open seats, and when comparing female challengers to male challengers. As the authors point out, "The problem for women candidates is not sex but incumbency. Incumbents, most of whom are men, win much more often than challengers. For women to have a level playing field, they have to wait for men to retire, resign, or die, and then run for the open seat."[14] Other studies have shown that congressional districts with women representatives tend to (1) have open-seat opportunities, (2) have a history of female candidates and representatives, and (3) exist mostly outside the South.[15] Women also tend to face more competition in primaries for seats in the US House of Representatives, although they do not win primaries at lower rates than their male counterparts.[16]

These factors help to explain the success that women had in 1992, dubbed by the news media as "The Year of the Woman." Several factors contributed to the "extraordinary opportunities for newcomers" that year, including an unusually large number of open seats resulting from retirements and redistricting based on the 1990 census. US voters were also in a strong anti-incumbent mood following public scandals involving the House of Representatives post office and bank. And women's groups were particularly motivated to nominate and elect women candidates following the Supreme Court confirmation hearings of Clarence Thomas (as discussed in Chapter 5). In this watershed election, women candidates won a record number of seats in both the House and the Senate. In the House, 106 women ran for congressional seats on a major party ticket, and forty-seven won seats in the general election. In the Senate, eleven women ran and six were elected, which contributed to the largest-ever one-time increase in candidates and winners. Gains were also made in state legislatures; prior to 1992, women made up 6 percent of Congress and 18 percent of state legislatures, with those numbers increasing to 10 percent in Congress and 20 percent at the state level following the 1992 election.[17]

Money in US politics, and more specifically how to regulate it, has been a prominent national issue for decades. Since Congress first passed the Federal Election Campaign Act in 1971—followed by major amendments to the act in 1974, many Supreme Court rulings, and constant political battles to pass additional legislation limiting the impact of money on campaigns— women candidates have developed effective strategies to raise enough money to fund their campaigns. When the number of women emerging as candidates for political office first started to increase in the 1970s, women struggled to raise adequate campaign funds. Most political observers assumed that since women were underrepresented in both politics (political action committees or PACs give proportionately more money to incumbents) and the corporate world (where many large single donations come from), they were at a huge disadvantage in terms of fundraising. Most also assumed that potential donors were reluctant to give money to women candidates and that women were "psychologically less predisposed to ask for donations." However, analyses of campaign funds raised and spent by women candidates show that by the 1990s, women were raising and spending as much or more than their male counterparts—and that women can and do win elected office when they choose to run. According to political scientist Barbara Burrell, "The new story is [women's] emergence as operators and leaders in the financing of campaigns for public office."[18] This is, however, an area in which incumbents still enjoy a sizable advantage over challengers; regardless of sex, challengers have a more difficult time raising money because they are often not seen as competitive.

As discussed in Chapter 3, women's PACs have made important financial contributions to women candidates in addition to providing training, consultation, and personnel in support of the campaign. The timing of financial contributions also plays an important role as "early money" is seen as crucial for women candidates in securing their party's nomination for the general election. EMILY's List for Democratic prochoice women candidates, the WISH List for Republican prochoice women candidates, and the Susan B. Anthony List for Republican prolife women candidates have all provided essential early money to women candidates. This helps to "establish a campaign's viability and signals other contributors" to also give money, and can be crucial for nonincumbent women candidates. (However, women's PACs give early money disproportionately to Democratic candidates, whereas Republican candidates "face a more daunting task of establishing early viability."[19]) EMILY's List also pioneered the strategy known as *bundling*, or gathering campaign contributions from friends and associates. Donors write their checks to the candidate's campaign fund, but the bundler takes credit for a large contribution to the campaign while avoiding the Federal Election Campaign limit on contributions to federal candidates. Based on the campaign finance laws passed in 2002 governing federal elections (which includes congressional campaigns), donors in the 2009–2010 campaign cycle were limited to contributions of $2,400 per election. But an individual or PAC can solicit contributions on behalf of a candidate and bundle them together to make one large (and legal) contribution to the campaign.

Although further analysis of women candidates and fund-raising is needed, it has become apparent that women running for Congress have matched and at times outpaced their male counterparts. For example, Senators Barbara Boxer (D) and Dianne Feinstein (D), along with Representative Jane Harmon (D), all of California, are known as prolific fund-raisers; Boxer and Feinstein ranked one and two, respectively, in 1992 among top fund-raisers for US Senate seats. Two years later, Feinstein raised another $11 million in successfully defending her Senate seat against millionaire Congressman Michael Huffington (who spent $30 million on his campaign). In the 1998 congressional elections, ten of the top fifty fund-raisers in the House of Representatives were women candidates, and eleven of the top fifty fund-raisers in 2000 were women. Whether or not donations by women have contributed to this trend is still unclear, but fund-raising within the women's community (particularly from national women's PACs) has played a significant role in the level of success in this area of campaigning.[20] The recent success among women candidates of both parties for congressional seats may be an important harbinger for women presidential candidates. Elizabeth Dole cited a lack of money for her early departure from the Republican presidential primaries in late 1999, but the fund-raising data from more recent congressional campaign cycles "seems to suggest that the traditional economic structural barriers to a woman running for the presidency are beginning to dissipate."[21] In fact, Hillary Rodham Clinton raised a total of $223 million for her presidential campaign in the primaries alone, a sum second only to the $750 million raised by Barack Obama during his entire presidential campaign. Despite losing the Democratic nomination to Obama, Clinton shattered any myth that women candidates cannot raise enough money to fund a campaign.

■ Media Coverage of Women Candidates

Despite the increased number of women winning elected office since the 1990s, women politicians are often still viewed by the press as an anomaly.[22] Trivialization of women in the news media (as discussed in Chapter 3) has also continued, as well as the stereotyping that occurs in news coverage of women candidates and politicians.[23] Studies have shown that news media coverage has added to the negative stereotyping of women candidates, thus hurting their efforts to win an elected office. According to political scientist Kim Fridkin Kahn, the news media pays more attention to style over substance when covering female candidates. Since voters may doubt the policy qualifications of women candidates, news coverage that downplays issues and highlights personal traits can lead to the development of less favorable images for female candidates. Also, traditionally male issues (the economy, defense, foreign policy) are highlighted during US Senate campaigns, whereas traditionally female issues (education, health care) are emphasized in gubernatorial races. Kahn suggests that female candidates have an advantage in discussing these issues, and from the subsequent media coverage, during gubernatorial races but that women candidates for the Senate should ignore the instinct to alter the accepted male agenda to consider supposed female issues, since by "demonstrating their competence in 'male' issues at a time when these issues are salient to the public, women candidates may be able to eradicate potentially damaging sex stereotypes." Women candidates also need to stress supposedly male traits, such as competence and leadership, during their campaigns.[24]

Other studies have found similar results. For example, in a study of several gubernatorial candidates, the White House Project (a nonpartisan organization dedicated to placing more women in top leadership positions within government and business) found not only that women candidates received more coverage regarding their style than substance but also that male reporters more often focused on personal angles than did female reporters. Furthermore, "reporters were more likely to highlight male candidates' positions and records on the issues and were more likely to quote male candidates' reasoning behind their claims."[25] The results of a similar study on women candidates in US Senate races supported the contention that news media coverage on television "disadvantaged women candidates in the eyes of voters" by providing more favorable coverage of male candidates than of women candidates.[26] However, although these studies and others show that media biases and negative stereotypes of women candidates still exist, "it does appear that coverage is becoming more equitable" in terms of quantity and substance.[27]

Still, according to journalism professor Maria Braden, subtle sex discrimination still exists. Our media-saturated political environment demands that image play a large role for both officeholders and office seekers, and it continues to be one of the most pressing problems faced by women running for high public office due to a long-held double standard in the press to insert details about appearance in news stories about women politicians but not in stories about men:

> More than a century later, women politicians are still discovering what [Susan B.] Anthony had learned—that journalists often ask women politicians questions they don't ask men. That reporters describe women politicians in ways and with words that emphasize women's traditional roles and focus on their appearance and behavior. That they perpetuate stereotypes of women politicians as weak, indecisive, and emotional. That they hold women politicians accountable for the actions of their children and husbands, though they rarely hold men to the same standards. . . . When the news media imply that women are anomalies in high public office, the public is likely to regard them as bench warmers rather than as an integral part of government.[28]

Women politicians can also be trivialized by the gender-specific words journalists commonly use to describe them, such as "plucky," "spunky," or "feisty."[29] While more research on the effects of negative and/or sexist coverage of women candidates and politicians is needed, particularly as the number and type of media outlets continue to expand, the studies to date suggest that the news media rarely portray women as authoritative and legitimate leaders within the political system. This is a particularly important issue for women candidates to face given the mass media's powerful role in the current political environment.[30]

This issue is particularly salient when considering women presidential candidates. Although much research has been conducted on how the news media portray presidential candidates and how it may impact the outcome of presidential elections, the role of gender is difficult to determine since so few women have run for office at the national level. We do know that during Geraldine Ferraro's run for the vice presidency in 1984 (with Democratic nominee Walter Mondale) and Elizabeth Dole's short-lived campaign for the Republican nomination in 1999 and 2000, gender was a significant label in the news coverage of both women candidates. Studies found that "the most pernicious coverage for both campaigns was the 'lipstick watch,'" with almost 30 percent of Ferraro's coverage and more than 40 percent of Dole's coverage containing references to clothing, makeup, hair, and other feminine categorizations.[31] Other studies suggest that although the news media is usually quick to herald the fact that US voters seem ready to elect a woman president, women running for elected office at all levels of government are still viewed as a political anomaly, that a disproportionate amount of coverage is devoted to clothing and hairstyles, and that the mass media in general still often rely on negative stereotypes of women.[32]

More definitive results than exist at the time of this writing in 2009 will eventually be available on the question of gender bias in presidential campaigns, beginning with the numerous studies that will be conducted on Hillary Rodham Clinton's 2008 presidential campaign. Initial assessments suggest that Clinton's status as the first viable female presidential candidate served as a double-edged sword for her candidacy. On the one hand, Clinton's campaign brought the nation extremely close to nominating a woman for a major party ticket for the first time, and the historic nature of that accomplishment helped to generate tremendous interest. Clinton also benefited from media coverage from 2005 to 2007 that declared her the presumptive frontrunner, virtually unstoppable in her quest for the nomination. On the other hand, Clinton was not immune from the negative stereotyping that exists for women politicians. Still, gender did not play as prominent a role in the campaign as some expected it would, as many discussions often revolved around "Hillary Clinton" running for president rather than a woman running for president, due to Clinton's name recognition and star power.

Thus, the emerging assessment of Clinton's portrayal in the news media is a complicated one. For another example, an early study of news during the 2007 invisible primary by the Project for Excellence in Journalism shows that Clinton had more coverage than any other candidate in either party, yet 38 percent of that coverage was negative, compared to just 27 percent positive (the remainder is considered neutral).[33] Many charges have been made about gender bias and sexism in campaign coverage, with some high-profile commentators—most notably Chris Matthews, Mike Barnicle, and Pat Buchanan in separate incidents on MSNBC—making questionable comments about Clinton's campaign based on gender, and future academic studies will show a better and more-detailed picture than the mostly anecdotal evidence available to date. However, based on the latter, the gender bias that did exist in news coverage often followed other trends in recent years for other female candidates.[34]

Media coverage of the entire 2008 presidential election is also unique due to the length of the campaign, the intense interest among Americans in it, and the ever-expanding means of communication (for example, blogging and social networking sites played a prominent role in coverage). Although future studies will probably find that Clinton did not escape some of the usual trends for covering women candidates, the sheer amount of coverage of the presidential campaign in 2008 may dilute findings of gender bias a bit. It is also important to point out that it is now acceptable, even expected, for news outlets to cover more issues of style (as opposed to issues of substance, like policy matters) for all candidates, male or female, than ever before. Examples from 2007 include the focus on former Senator John Edwards's US$400 haircut and a story in the *New York Times* on the candidates' eating habits and exercise routines on the campaign trail (with particular attention given to New Mexico governor Bill Richardson's struggles with his weight).[35] This fits the trend in recent years for "soft" versus "hard" news.[36]

In the final analysis, determining whether news coverage of Clinton had a detrimental effect on her campaign is not a simple proposition. An interesting question arises over whether Clinton is really a good test case for determining gender bias in campaign coverage, since some may have been more negatively biased against "Hillary as Hillary" (and wife of Bill Clinton) than against Clinton as a woman running for president. Obviously, the two cannot be separated entirely, but it puts the question into a unique context and perspective as scholars continue to assess the 2008 presidential campaign. In addition, the media sensation that Sarah Palin became when she was first introduced as John McCain's running mate in September 2008 provides an interesting case study about how women candidates are treated once arriving on the national stage. Like Clinton's, Palin's relationship with the news media was unique due to her political persona, her life story, and her political ideology; but even so, much attention was paid to both her appearance and her family. Many more women presidential and vice presidential candidates will need to emerge before a standard can be set when it comes to covering women on the national campaign trail. In all likelihood, a determination will not be made until we see the next woman running for president to know if real progress has been made on the gender issue in presidential campaign news coverage.

■ **Conclusion**

How we elect politicians in the United States plays an important role in determining the number of women who serve in public office. Although women candidates, especially when running for Congress, have succeeded in recent years in the area of fundraising, the incumbency advantage still hurts the chances of any new or outsider candidate, but particularly women and minorities, from winning seats and thereby possibly bringing a different perspective to the policymaking process. And although women officeholders may not be quite the novelty that they once were,

Geraldine Ferraro and the News Media:
A Long and Winding Road

Type in the name Geraldine Ferraro on any Internet search engine, and you will find Web page after Web page that calls her a "political leader"[37] who "forever reshaped the American political and social landscape."[38] Although many young women today may not be familiar with Ferraro or her historic run for the vice presidency in 1984, she remains an important symbol in US politics for older generations of women who saw her as a groundbreaking candidate on the national level. The first woman to be nominated on a major party ticket, the congresswoman from Queens, New York, would also be the test case for the news media on how to handle a female candidate on the presidential campaign trail.

In her six-year tenure in the House of Representatives, Ferraro had gained a reputation for pursuing legislation beneficial to women's causes, including working for passage of the Equal Rights Amendment, sponsoring the Women's Economic Equity Act ending pension discrimination against women, and seeking greater job training and opportunities for displaced homemakers. In 1984, under pressure from women's rights advocates and women's organizations such as the National Organization for Women to place a woman on the ticket, Democratic presidential nominee Walter Mondale made history by picking Ferraro as his running mate. In spite of her strong reputation as a legislator, Ferraro was considered a gamble by some political analysts, but a necessary one for Mondale to have any chance of upsetting incumbent president Ronald Reagan that November. To Democrats, Ferraro represented the candidate who could close the gender gap; by the summer months of 1983, polls showed that 17 percent fewer women than men supported the president and his policies, leading party leaders to believe that the powerful voting bloc of women could make the difference. Instead, Reagan walked away with a resounding victory, winning every state except Mondale's home of Minnesota.

Although the race between Mondale and Reagan was not close by the fall of 1984, Ferraro's presence on the ticket as the "first" woman vice presidential candidate made headlines right up until election day. One of the biggest stories of the campaign became the business dealings of Ferraro's husband, John Zaccaro. When Ferraro revealed that her husband had decided not to release his tax returns because it might compromise his business dealings, the press had a field day. Never before had a candidate's spouse been subjected to such scrutiny by the press. In her book about the campaign, *Ferraro: My Story*, Ferraro recalls stating at a press conference, "He's not the candidate, I am." More than 250 reporters

continues

jammed the "disclosure" press conference only to learn that both Ferraro and her husband had overpaid, not underpaid, their federal income taxes.[39] The scrutiny by the press would continue throughout the campaign, on issues ranging from Ferraro's views on abortion as a Catholic (she was prochoice) to how a "lady" candidate was supposed to act (for example, should she and Mondale hug in public or merely shake hands?) to whether or not, due to her Italian heritage, her family had ties to organized crime (no evidence ever surfaced). Ferraro also recalled that conservative columnist George Will of the *Washington Post* wrote a scathing column about her family finances prior to the press conference at which the tax returns were disclosed. Ferraro challenged him on a national news show, saying he would have to apologize when the tax forms were revealed. Instead, Will sent her a dozen roses with a card that read, "Has anyone told you you are cute when you're mad?"[40]

Throughout the campaign, novel—and somewhat odd—stories about Ferraro kept appearing. Even before the Democratic convention had come to a close, the *Los Angeles Times* ran a column titled "Convention Notebook" that included an interesting commentary on a new problem Mondale and Ferraro would face: with so many Secret Service agents around, which candidate would go down the elevator first and be forced to wait in the garage for the other? The headline gave away the answer, "During Drafty Delay in a Garage, Protocol Rules It's Ladies First."[41] Many media outlets also could not help but talk about fashion in their political reporting. The *New York Times*'s story on Ferraro's nomination described her appearance and clothing three separate times. Starting with "Mrs. Ferraro, dressed in a white suit, gave the thumbs-up sign in response to the convention," the story continued with a reference to Ferraro's appearance at a fund-raiser earlier in the day, "dressed in a bright turquoise dress," and called speaker of the House Tip O'Neill's comments about Ferraro "avuncular." The third reference to appearance stated that Ferraro was "clad in white and wearing a string of pearls about her neck" while "bounc[ing] in time to the beat of the song, 'New York, New York,' as, with a broad grin, she accepted waves of applause." The news of Ferraro hugging several House colleagues whom she had not seen since Mondale had announced her candidacy was also included in the story.[42] Ferraro's campaign, and resulting relationship with the press, also got off to an auspicious start during an August appearance in Mississippi. Jim Buck Ross, the state agriculture commissioner, quizzed Ferraro on whether or not she could bake blueberry muffins. When she responded, "I sure can. Can you?" she was informed that men in the South don't cook. The exchange made headlines for several days in newspapers across the nation.[43]

continues

After the loss in 1984, Ferraro would not return to politics until 1992, when she sought the Democratic nomination in New York for the US Senate. One of four candidates for the nomination, Ferraro believed that much of the press coverage focusing on her novelty as the first woman to run for vice president and attacking her family were behind her. However, allegations concerning her husband's business connections and questions about their tax returns surfaced again. The stories once again made national headlines, this time mostly due to the identity of her accuser—one of her challengers for the nomination, New York comptroller and former congresswoman Elizabeth Holtzman. Like Ferraro, Holtzman was known as a feminist politician supportive of women's rights, and had beaten a veteran incumbent in 1972 to first get elected to Congress. Trailing Ferraro in the early polls, Holtzman went on the attack using negative television ads—as many candidates do—in an attempt to slow down the frontrunner's momentum. But a feminist woman attacking another feminist woman was too good a story for the national press to pass up, revealing a unique double standard to the effect that "the women weren't acting the way women were supposed to act," since they were behaving more like male politicians.[44] In the end, neither Ferraro nor Holtzman earned the Democratic nomination, and New York would not participate in the "Year of the Woman" by sending its first elected woman to the Senate; that would not happen until Hillary Rodham Clinton's election in 2000.

Ferraro again ran unsuccessfully for the US Senate in 1998, losing the Democratic nomination to the eventual winner of the seat, Representative Charles Schumer. From 1996 to 1998, Ferraro cohosted the CNN show *Crossfire* as a representative of the political left, and she continues to provide political commentary as a frequent guest on national television news programs. She also made headlines during the 2008 presidential campaign; an early supporter of Hillary Rodham Clinton, Ferraro caused a stir when she commented on the success of Barack Obama's campaign during the Democratic primaries: "If Obama [were] a white man, he would not be in this position. And if he [were] a woman (of any color) he would not be in this position. He happens to be very lucky to be who he is. And the country is caught up in the concept."[45] Ferraro was accused by many of making a racist comment, whereas she insisted that she was only speaking about historic candidacies. Nonetheless, within days of the story, she resigned her position on the Clinton campaign finance committee. On the nomination of Sarah Palin as the second woman to run on a major party ticket for vice president, Ferraro stated her pleasure in no longer being the only woman to run for the office: "Every time a woman runs, women win."[46]

negative stereotyping in news coverage of women candidates persists. In order for more women to be elected to public office, they must be encouraged to do so by political parties and other political activists; perhaps more important, they need to believe that they have a strong chance of winning. Feminist/prochoice women candidates made substantial gains in both congressional and state races in 1992, but it is worth noting that two years later, in 1994 (dubbed the "Year of the Angry White Male" as the Republican Party captured both houses of Congress for the first time in forty years), several conservative, prolife women were also elected to Congress, reminding us that a monolithic group of women politicians does not exist. Since the mid-1990s, the gains for women winning elections to public offices at all levels of government have slowed down tremendously, with only modest and incremental increases. Perhaps future research by political scientists and other interested observers should continue to consider what changes to both public institutions and public policy result from women at both ends of the political/ideological spectrum running for, and eventually holding, public office.

■ Study/Discussion Questions

1. What factors contribute to the successful recruitment of women candidates? Why, even given successful examples, do some women still believe that they cannot win an election?

2. How do party leaders and other political activists impact the recruitment of women candidates? What can they do to encourage more women to run for public office?

3. What role does incumbency play in congressional elections, and why is it such an imposing barrier for women candidates?

4. Why is early money so important for women candidates, and how have women's PACs helped to alleviate the financial burden of campaigning?

5. In what ways does the news media perpetuate negative stereotypes of both women candidates and women politicians?

6. How does Geraldine Ferraro's historic run for the vice presidency in 1984 compare to the 2008 campaigns of Hillary Rodham Clinton and Sarah Palin? Will future female presidential and vice presidential candidates face similar challenges?

■ Online Resources

Accuracy in Media. http://www.aim.org.
Center for Media and Public Affairs. http://www.cmpa.com.
Democratic Senatorial Campaign Committee. http://www.dscc.org.
Federal Election Commission. http://www.fec.gov.
House Democratic Campaign Committee. http://www.hdcc.org.
National Republican Congressional Committee. http://www.nrcc.org.
National Republican Senatorial Committee. http://www.nrsc.org.
OpenSecrets.org. http://www.opensecrets.org.

■ Notes

1. See McGlen et al., *Women, Politics, and American Society*, 90–102.
2. Darcy, Welch, and Clark, *Women, Elections, and Representation*, 15–18.
3. Mandel, "A Question About Women and the Leadership Option," 72.
4. Darcy, Welch, and Clark, *Women, Elections, and Representation*, 27–28.
5. Carroll, *Women as Candidates in American Politics*, 42–44.
6. Darcy, Welch, and Clark, *Women, Elections, and Representation*, 175–176.
7. See Sanbonmatsu, "Candidate Recruitment and Women's Election to the State Legislatures."
8. Carroll, *Women as Candidates in American Politics*, 91.
9. Duerst-Lahti, "The Bottleneck," 15.
10. See Elder, "Why Women Don't Run."
11. See Fox and Lawless, "Entering the Arena?"
12. See Fox, "The Future of Women's Political Leadership," 251–270.
13. Carroll, *Women as Candidates in American Politics*, 119.
14. Seltzer, Newman, and Leighton, *Sex as a Political Variable*, 7.
15. Ondercin and Welch, "Women Candidates for Congress," 60–80.
16. See Lawless and Pearson, "The Primary Reason for Women's Underrepresentation?"
17. Thomas, "Introduction," 6–8.
18. Burrell, "Campaign Finance," 26–40.
19. See Francia, "Early Fundraising by Nonincumbent Female Congressional Candidates."
20. Burrell, "Money and Women's Candidacies for Public Office," 82.

21. Farrar-Myers, "A War Chest Full of Susan B. Anthony Dollars," 92.
22. Rice, "Women Out of the Myths and into Focus," 45–49.
23. See Tuchman, *Hearth and Home*, 7–8, and Paletz, *The Media in American Politics*, 135–139.
24. Kahn, *The Political Consequences of Being a Woman*, 134-136.
25. Wilson, *Closing the Leadership Gap*, 37–38.
26. See Kropf and Boiney, "The Electoral Glass Ceiling?"
27. Bystrom et al., *Gender and Candidate Communication*, 21.
28. See Braden, *Women Politicians and the Media*, 1–4.
29. Braden, *Women Politicians and the Media*, 6–7.
30. Kahn, "Assessing the Media's Impact on the Political Fortunes of Women," 173–189.
31. Heith, "The Lipstick Watch," 124–126.
32. Many studies on this topic have been conducted in recent years. For example, see Paletz, *The Media in American Politics*, 135–139; Kahn, *The Political Consequences of Being a Woman*, 134–136; Kropf and Boiney, "The Electoral Glass Ceiling?" 21; and Heldman, Carroll, and Olson, "'She Brought Only a Skirt.'"
33. "The Invisible Primary—Invisible No Longer: A First Look at Coverage of the 2008 Presidential Campaign."
34. See Seelye and Bosman, "Media Charged with Sexism in Clinton Coverage," 1.
35. Kantor, "Where the Votes Are, So, Unfortunately, Are All Those Calories," A1.
36. Soft news is defined as news having no real connection to substantive policy issues, or as the opposite of hard news, which includes coverage of breaking events and major issues impacting the daily routines of US citizens; it has steadily increased since the 1990s in response to competition in the marketplace. See Patterson, "Doing Well and Doing Good."
37. Infoplease, "Geraldine Anne Ferraro."
38. National Women's Hall of Fame. "Geraldine Ferraro: Women of the Hall."
39. Ferraro and Francke, *Ferraro: My Story*, 174–180.
40. Ibid., 179–180.
41. "Convention Notebook," A7.
42. Perlez, "'Gerry, Gerry,' the Convention Chants," A1.
43. Weinraub, "Mississippi Farm Topic," 16.
44. Braden, *Women Politicians and the Media*, 134.
45. Farber, "Geraldine Ferraro Lets Her Emotions Do the Talking."
46. Baird, "From Seneca Falls to . . . Sarah Palin?"

5

Women as Legislators

Some things will still be unfinished when you die. But if you keep at it and lay the foundation and bring others in, they'll carry on.

■ US senator Dianne Feinstein (D-California)

In recent years, women have made great strides in getting elected to legislative positions at both the federal and state level. These seats of power within the US system of government are crucial to policymaking, as legislators are directly responsible for writing the laws at all levels of government. There are now more women serving in the US Congress and in state legislatures across the country than ever before. At the start of the 111th Session of Congress in 2009, three states (California, Maine, and Washington) held the distinction of being represented by two women in the US Senate, long regarded as an exclusive all-male club in Washington, D.C. And in the House of Representatives, Nancy Pelosi (D-California) made history in 2007 with her election to the top leadership post as speaker of the House, the highest—and only—leadership position in Congress ever held by a woman.

But despite the progress in the past decade or so, women are still nowhere close to reaching parity with men as members of Congress or state legislators. As discussed in Chapter 1, women still make up only roughly 17 percent of Congress and 24 percent of state legislatures. This represents an important paradox for women, who make up 51 percent of the voting population: how to translate that voting strength into proportional representation within state and national government? Why has the progress in getting women elected to legislative positions been so slow? And when women do get elected to office, why do so few rise to leadership positions within the party ranks? As we discussed in Chapter 4 and will continue to discuss here, women have traditionally faced unique barriers during their pursuit of legislative careers. Another important question to consider concerns the leadership style of women legislators, and whether or not it makes a difference in terms of both the policymaking process and policy outcomes. In this chapter, we discuss women and legislative leadership, the history of women serving in Congress, the impact of women legislators on the policy agenda, and the number and impact of women serving in state legislatures.

■ Women and Legislative Leadership

Why study women as legislators, and what can we learn about women's style of leadership in the legislature? First, it is important to understand how a legislature functions to achieve its ultimate goal of lawmaking. Individual members of a legislature are elected to represent an equal number of citizens (or, in the case of the US Senate, states are represented equally with two members each) in the policymaking process. While some members may have more seniority or may be members of the majority party, which may in turn provide them more powerful committee or leadership positions, all legislatures within the United States operate on the simple premise of "one person, one vote." In most areas of the decisionmaking process, a simple majority among the members in both houses is required to pass a bill that is then sent to the executive branch to be signed or vetoed by the president or state governor. (Exceptions in Congress include, for example, a two-thirds vote to override a presidential veto or to approve a constitutional amendment to then be considered by the states.) As a result, consensus building and cooperation among members is necessary to pass legislation.

Cindy Simon Rosenthal, in her study of women state legislators, explains that the study of legislative leadership has mostly considered men and as a result has failed to acknowledge the contribution of women to lawmaking. "Congressional studies, which dominate the legislative literature, remain mostly about men. Might it be that male behavior has been conflated as institutional behavior?"[1] If women traditionally exhibit leadership traits that are more openly democratic and cooperative and that promote a group-centered mode of decisionmaking, then, one might assume, women have a positive impact on how legislatures function. Rosenthal's study, which consists of surveys of legislative committee chairs from fifty states, focus groups, interviews, and an extensive study of the state legislatures in Colorado, Ohio, and Oklahoma, demonstrates that "sex, the social understandings of gender, and gendered institutions all influence leadership style."[2] She categorizes legislative leadership into two distinct styles: *aggregative* (also known as *transactional*), which is leader-centered, hierarchical (with leaders exercising power over others), and *integrative* (also known as *transformational*), which is nonhierarchical, stressing mutuality, community, and the empowerment of others (and a common purpose among members).[3] Aggregative/transactional leadership is considered by researchers to be the norm within legislatures, in part due to the fact that they have historically been dominated by men. However, as women have gained a more prominent role, the integrative/transformational leadership style has been increasingly visible in legislatures, yet researchers have mostly ignored this trend until very recently.

In examining institutions in which both men and women occupy leadership roles, modest differences in leadership traits among men and women become apparent. For example, women committee chairs often exhibit leadership styles closer to the integrative/transformational model. As Rosenthal states, "Leadership is a complex phenomenon of individual experiences, circumstances, and relationships. Nonetheless, on a wide variety of individual measures of leadership traits, motivation, or behavior, women and men differ in ways that are substantively and statistically significant."[4] In a later writing, Rosenthal also concludes there is evidence from states across the nation to indicate that "women committee chairs in state legislatures adopt styles that emphasize both getting things done and getting along, but that getting things done predominates." And although women legislators are becoming more assertive leaders, their continued effectiveness and inclusion within the institutional setting demands that more women achieve leadership positions.[5]

■   **Women in Congress: A History**

Since the first session of Congress in 1789, nearly 12,000 people have served in the national legislature. Of those, only 2 percent have been women.[6] The main argument put forth by suffragists in the struggle to secure the vote for women centered on the arguments that women should not be prevented from civic participation and duties and that women should be allowed to select their own representatives. So when women did secure the right to vote with the ratification of the Nineteenth Amendment to the US Constitution in 1920, many assumed that women would voice their political preferences by electing other women. However, as discussed in Chapter 3, not all women rushed to the ballot box to participate in the electoral process. Other factors came into play as well to contribute to the many obstacles that women politicians would face in the following decades. Few women actually sought elective office during the first half of the twentieth century, and of those who did, several were nominated by the minority party in a particular district where the candidate had little chance of winning.

The first woman to serve in the US Congress was actually elected before women nationwide had the right to vote. Jeannette Rankin, a Republican from Montana, served two terms in the US House of Representatives, the first from 1917 to 1918 (Montana had granted women's suffrage prior to 1920) and the second from 1941 to 1942. Rankin, a pacifist, was the only member of Congress to vote against US entry into both World War I and World War II. Rebecca Latimer Felton, a Georgia Democrat in her eighties, became the first woman to serve in the US Senate in 1922. She was appointed as a temporary replacement and only served for two days before giving up her seat to the man who had been elected to it. Hattie Wyatt Caraway, an Arkansas Democrat who was appointed to the US Senate to succeed her late husband in 1931, was the first of many women to take this path to the Senate. Caraway would later become the first woman ever elected to the Senate in her own right, where she served two full terms. She was also the first woman to chair a Senate committee—the minor position of chair of the Committee on Enrolled Bills.

While women succeeding to the Congress as widows was a common occurrence throughout the twentieth century, it is now more often the exception than the rule. When a vacancy occurs in the House of Representatives, a special election must be held. In the Senate, a vacancy is usually filled through a gubernatorial appointment until the next regularly scheduled federal election (which occurs in every even-numbered year). However, three more recent examples show that the practice of installing widows, who have the advantage of name recognition, is still in effect. Doris Matsui, widow of twenty-six-year House veteran Robert Matsui, won a special election to her late husband's district in California in March 2005. Mary Bono, the widow of entertainer and former Palm Springs, California, mayor Sonny Bono, won a special election to fill his House seat upon his accidental death in 1998. And in the Senate, Jean Carnahan represented the state of Missouri for two years after her husband posthumously won election in 2002. Mel Carnahan, a Democrat, died in a plane crash two weeks prior to the election, where he was challenging the incumbent Republican senator John Ashcroft. His wife Jean was then appointed to fill the Senate seat by the state governor, but she lost her reelection bid in 2004.

Major growth in the number of women seeking and gaining legislative office at the national level did not occur until the late 1960s and early 1970s. The modern women's movement began to change the political environment, albeit slowly, by encouraging more women to seek political office in an effort to change public policies that affected them directly. One woman who arrived in Congress during this period was Patricia Schroeder, who served twenty-four years in the House of Representatives as a Democrat from Colorado. Schroeder was elected to Congress in 1972 at the age of 32. Her first campaign, run out of her own house, focused on ideas rather than money. She beat the political odds to win the seat, since her campaign was as short on political support and endorsements as it was on cash. The only endorsements she received came from the few African American elected officials in Colorado at the time. Not only did the Democratic Party refuse to support her campaign, but the Colorado Women's Political Caucus, which she had helped to found, also denied her an endorsement. The average campaign contribution was a mere $7.50, which came from several individual supporters within the congressional district.[7] Schroeder, who defied the critics and naysayers when she first got elected, always maintained a leadership style based on her outsider status, as opposed to the many women she would later see in Congress who tried to move things along and play by the rules: "It's not that they lack vision, but they want to remain players. Whereas I arrived realizing I would *never* be a player—so I would play the outsider game."[8]

By 1984, the number of women nominated by their party to run for the House of Representatives had increased dramatically. A total of sixty-five women ran for the House that year; however, only twenty-two women were elected, and most who won were incumbents. Meanwhile, Representative Geraldine Ferraro of New York became Democrat Walter Mondale's running mate in the presidential election. But many political observers concluded that although Ferraro's candidacy had been symbolically important for women, real progress, reflected in the number of women elected, had not occurred.

In 1986, Barbara Mikulski of Maryland became the first Democratic woman to be elected to the Senate without having first been appointed to the seat. Mikulski, who is now known as a master strategist in getting bills passed, spent her early years in the Senate learning as much about the institution and its processes as possible. She also respected Senate traditions and rules, seeking the guidance and advice of the Democratic men with whom she served:

> I was at an initial disadvantage as a woman coming to the Senate, and it wasn't just that the gym was off-limits. I didn't come to politics by the traditional male route, being in a nice law firm or belonging to the right clubs. Like most of the women I've known in politics, I got involved because I saw a community need. And it was tough, absolutely. I didn't have any natural mentors to show me the ropes. I had to seek out my mentors. So when four women finally joined me in the Senate in 1993, I was very gratified. I gladly took on the role of mentor and adviser.[9]

In 1991, a nomination to the US Supreme Court became a catalyst among women seeking office, triggering as well a grassroots effort among women's advocacy groups to change the gender balance on Capitol Hill. When President George H.W. Bush nominated Clarence Thomas to fill a vacancy on the Supreme Court due to the retirement of Associate Justice Thurgood Marshall, no one could have predicted the national firestorm over sexual harassment that would be unleashed. When law professor Anita Hill's claims of sexual harassment against Thomas, for whom she had worked at the Equal Employment Opportunity Commission, were leaked to the press, Hill was called to testify before the all-male Senate Judiciary Committee. Prior to the investigation into the charges, it was unclear as to whether the Senate would take the accusations seriously.

Seven women in the House of Representatives were outraged over the apparent indifference to such a charge by their male colleagues in the Senate. On October 8, 1991—then-members of the House Barbara Boxer (D-CA), Louise Slaughter (D-NY), Eleanor Holmes-Norton (D-DC), Nita Lowey (D-NY), Patsy Mink (D-HI), and Jolene Unsoeld (D-WA), led by Schroeder and accompanied by several reporters—marched up the steps to the Senate on the opposite side of the Capitol to demand that their concerns be heard by the Democratic leadership. Boxer recalled later that the women wanted to help Democratic senators, who were attending their regular Tuesday Democratic caucus lunch, understand the importance of the issue. At the time, only two women (Mikulski and Nancy Kassebaum, a Republican from Kansas) were serving in the Senate. The women believed that their perspective would be welcomed; instead, they initially found themselves outside a closed door they were not allowed to enter. Finally, with the threat of negative press coverage from the reporters present, Senate majority leader George Mitchell agreed to meet with the women in a side room.

Further testimony and investigations did follow into Hill's allegations against Thomas. However, Thomas was confirmed by the full Senate in a vote of 52–48 (the second-closest vote ever to confirm a Supreme Court nominee). Still, the event proved to be galvanizing in the sense that women across the nation realized the extent to which they were invisible among the political elite in Washington. Boxer recalled, "It was humiliating to be so summarily dismissed—to have to beg for a hearing. But we kept demanding to be heard until [Mitchell] agreed to meet with us. And so we got our hearing. It turned out to be a travesty. It was shameful. But it was also a wake-up call. All over the country, women watched those hearings and reacted to seeing that long row of white male senators. It was made painfully clear that they just 'didn't get it.'"[10]

As a result, the presidential and congressional election year of 1992 became known as "The Year of the Woman." Many more women ran for Congress than in years past due in part to the Hill-Thomas controversy. As a result, the number of women in Congress rose from thirty-two at the end of the 102nd Congress to fifty-two during the 103rd Congress, with twenty newly elected women in the House and four newly elected women in the Senate. (The new senators included Democrats Barbara Boxer and Dianne Feinstein of California, Patty Murray of Washington, and Carol Moseley Braun of Illinois; Republican Kay Bailey Hutchison of Texas increased the total number of women in the Senate to seven when she won a special election in June 1993 to replace Democrat Lloyd Bentsen, who had been appointed treasury secretary in the new Clinton administration.) More than sixty million women voted in the general election in November 1992, playing a crucial role in the largest increase of women elected to Congress in history. The success of women candidates in 1992 can also be attributed to many other factors, among them redistricting, a record number of retirements from the House, and the House post office and bank scandals in 1991 and 1992, respectively. These issues, as well as legislative gridlock between a Democratic-controlled Congress and a Republican White House, contributed to the public desire in 1992 for a change in the membership and policies on Capitol Hill. Women capitalized on this situation as relative newcomers "with a strong reputation for honesty and integrity on the one hand, and expertise on many domestic issues on the other," such that they "were looked upon to initiate reform."[11]

Since 1992, the number of women serving in Congress has steadily yet slowly increased. As of 2010, there are a total of ninety women serving in Congress—seventy-three in the House and seventeen in the Senate (see Tables 5.1 and 5.2). In addition, women hold three of the five nonvoting seats in the House (belonging to the District of Columbia, Guam, and the US Virgin Islands). Twenty-eight states are now represented by at least one woman in the House. Among the largest states, California has nineteen women representatives, New York six, Florida six, and Ohio five. Texas, the second-most-populous state in the nation, only has three women in its House delegation. Of the ninety congresswomen, a total of twenty-one (23.3 percent), all in the House, are women of color, ten of whom are members of the delegation of California, the most populous state in the nation, with the greatest racial and ethnic diversity among its citizens.[12]

Table 5.1   Women in the 111th Congress, US House of Representatives

State	No. of Women Representatives/Total	Percentage
Arizona	2/8	25.0
California	19/53	33.9
Colorado	2/7	28.6
Connecticut	1/5	20.0
Florida	6/25	24.0
Hawaii	1/2	50.0
Illinois	4/19	21.1
Kansas	1/4	25.0
Maine	1/2	50.0
Maryland	1/8	12.5
Massachusetts	1/10	10.0
Michigan	2/15	13.3
Minnesota	2/8	25.0
Missouri	1/9	11.1
Nevada	2/3	66.7
New Hampshire	1/2	50.0
New York	6/29	20.7
North Carolina	2/13	15.4
Ohio	5/18	27.8
Oklahoma	1/5	10.0
Pennsylvania	2/19	10.5
South Dakota	1/1	100.0
Tennessee	1/9	11.1
Texas	3/32	9.4
Washington	1/9	11.1
West Virginia	1/3	33.3
Wisconsin	2/8	25.0
Wyoming	1/1	100.0

Source: Center for American Women and Politics, Rutgers, The State University of New Jersey.

■ Women in Congress: The Policy Agenda

Studies since the early 1990s show that an increase of women in state legislatures, specifically in leadership positions with greater access to the news media, can positively impact the passage of legislation that affects women.[13] However, not all women in the Congress are homogeneous, either in terms of their style or the

Table 5.2   Women in the 111th Congress, US Senate

Senator	State (Party Affiliation)	Year Elected
Barbara Boxer	California (D)	1992
Maria Cantwell	Washington (D)	2000
Susan Collins	Maine (R)	1996
Dianne Feinstein	California (D)	1992
Kirsten Gillibrand[a]	New York (D)	2009
Kay Hagen	North Carolina (D)	2008
Kay Bailey Hutchison	Texas (R)	1993
Amy Klobuchar	Minnesota (D)	2006
Mary Landrieu	Louisiana (D)	1996
Blanche Lincoln	Arkansas (D)	1998
Claire McCaskill	Missouri (D)	2006
Barbara Mikulski	Maryland (D)	1986
Lisa Murkowski	Alaska (R)	2002
Patty Murray	Washington (D)	1992
Jeanne Shaheen	New Hampshire (D)	2008
Olympia Snowe	Maine (R)	1994
Debbie Stabenow	Michigan (D)	2000

Source: Center for American Women and Politics, Rutgers, The State University of New Jersey.
Note: a. Gillibrand was appointed to fill the vacant Senate seat of Hillary Rodham Clinton upon the latter's confirmation as secretary of state in January 2009.

substance of their policy agendas, yet most do "perceive of themselves as surrogate representatives for women and share some common perceptions about the experiences and ties that bind women together" regardless of party affiliation, political ideology, racial/ethnic background, or home district or state.[14] Studies show that women are "having a distinctive impact on the congressional agenda" at the federal level as well, where both Democratic and Republican women are "more likely to advocate women's issue bills than are their male partisan colleagues, particularly feminist legislation." However, the political environment in which women members of Congress find themselves can also impact the type of legislation they pursue; considerations also might include whether they have seniority on a given committee or whether their party is in the majority or the minority. The greatest diversity among women members of Congress in recent years has occurred among

Congresswoman Loretta Sanchez:
Playing by Her Own Rules

Representative Loretta Sanchez (D-CA) knows how to make head-lines. A political novice when she ran for the House of Representatives in 1996, she defeated an eighteen-year House veteran, the outspoken archconservative icon Robert Dornan, by a mere 984 votes. Dornan would not leave his seat quietly, accusing the Sanchez campaign of cheating by relying on the illegal votes of nonresident immigrants. A House investigation proved otherwise, and after lots of press attention on both the local and national level, Sanchez's political career began. In 1998, Sanchez handily beat Dornan in a rematch by 17 percent of the votes. In 2000, as cochair of the Democratic National Committee, Sanchez's plans to host a fund-raiser at the Playboy mansion in Los Angeles during the Democratic National Convention upset many party leaders; at first refusing to relocate the fund-raiser, Sanchez eventually changed her venue. In April 2001, while many of her congressional colleagues were postponing or canceling trips to China during the US spy plane standoff, Sanchez went ahead with the visit, accompanied by about a dozen other US lawmakers. And in 2003, Sanchez made history when her sister, Linda Sanchez, was also elected to the House of Representatives from California, making them the first sisters, and the first women of any relation, to serve in Congress. In 2008, the two published a joint memoir titled *Dream in Color: How the Sanchez Sisters Are Making History in Congress*.

Sanchez represents the 47th Congressional District of California, which includes the cities of Anaheim, Garden Grove, and Santa Ana as well as some of Fullerton in Orange County. One of seven children raised in Anaheim by immigrant parents from Mexico, Sanchez never intended to pursue a political career. In 1982, she earned a bachelor's degree in economics from Chapman University in Orange, California (where she was voted "Business Student of the Year"), going on to receive an MBA from American University in Washington, D.C. She then began a business career as a financial manager at the Orange County Transportation Authority, followed by consulting work—which included a position at Booz, Allen, and Hamilton, one of the top consulting firms in the nation. Sanchez then started her own consulting business in Santa Ana, California, assisting public agencies and private firms with financial matters, including cost-benefit analysis, strategic planning, and capital acquisition.[15]

continues

Congresswoman Loretta Sanchez *continued*

However, when the opportunity presented itself to run for the House in 1996 to represent the community in which she grew up, Sanchez relied on determination and a strong grassroots effort to win both the Democratic primary and the general election. The changing demographics in Orange County helped as well. Long known as a conservative Republican stronghold, the mostly upscale county south of Los Angeles on the California coastline had grown from a population of 400,000 to 2.8 million during the 1990s. In addition, Republican voter registration dropped from 55 to 49 percent during that time period, due in part to the loss of many middle-class aerospace jobs and a large wave of Latino and Asian immigrants who tended to vote Democratic. Sanchez's upset victory over Dornan in 1996 proved the point that Orange County was no longer dominated by its "reliably rock-solid, conservative, suburban, white, Republican vote—the kind of vote you could take to the bank, and which scores of [Republican] candidates did."[16]

Her supporters have called Sanchez a "dragon slayer" and a "modern-day Helen of Troy," not only for her upset victory over Dornan in 1996 but also for her tenaciousness and independence in representing her constituents.[17] A former Republican, she has been known to side with Republican colleagues on issues dealing with the economy or national security. Sanchez is the ranking woman on the House Armed Services Committee and was selected by Speaker Nancy Pelosi to serve as the vice chair of the House Committee on Homeland Security. In addition, she is the chairwoman of the Subcommittee on Border, Maritime, and Global Counterterrorism, the cochair of the Congressional Caucus on Vietnam, and a member of the Women's Congressional Caucus, the Blue Dog Democrats (a group of fiscally conservative House Democrats who tend to vote together as a coalition on budgetary and economic issues), the New Democratic Coalition (known as the moderate/centrist as opposed to liberal wing of the Democratic Party), and the Congressional Human Rights Caucus. Sanchez resigned from the Congressional Hispanic Caucus in 2007 after claiming that Representative Joe Baca (D-CA), chairman of the group, had referred to her in a derogatory manner; other women in the group also accused Baca of treating female members unfairly.[18]

Sanchez's leadership style focuses on community involvement and accessibility to constituents within her district. She travels

continues

Congresswoman Loretta Sanchez *continued*

home each week from Washington to hold what she calls "community office hours," meeting with constituents and generating community interest in key government issues. And in 2002, Sanchez was selected to serve as the first Latina member of Chapman University's board of trustees. As for future political aspirations, Sanchez has hinted that she may be interested in running for the US Senate; she even considered running for governor when California voters recalled incumbent Democrat Gray Davis in 2003. Regardless of what options may be in her political future—a statewide position in California or an even higher office—Sanchez has already proven herself a force to be reckoned with in the political arena.

Republican women, as the Republican Party has taken a more social conservative stance on many issues at the national level, a trend that has placed pressure on moderate Republican women who differ with the majority in their party on women's issues (for example, reproductive rights).[19]

As Senator Olympia Snowe points out, the women in the Senate are different "in our political positions, our styles, our life experiences. However, women just come from a different place than men do in terms of being more relationship oriented and more collaborative. In fact, many of the skills women develop in life actually work pretty well in this institution . . . where collaboration is an essential ingredient in getting things done."[20] Despite partisan affiliations, most women in the Congress have forged a sense of collegiality that comes from their experiences as women in a traditionally male-dominated institution. The women in the Senate, for example, get together for regular informal dinners in Washington. The purpose of the dinners is not behind-the-scenes deal making, but for engaging in a "familiar ritual among women colleagues everywhere—that uniquely female manner of lending support by sharing experiences, describing challenges, and talking about the issues they care about."[21]

The women in the House of Representatives have a more formal method of discussing important issues and collaborating on pieces of legislation dealing with women's issues. The

Congressional Caucus for Women's Issues, a bipartisan group founded in 1977, has fought for the passage of many bills dealing with economic, educational, and health care issues, among others. One of the biggest challenges the caucus has ever faced came in 1995, when Republicans gained control of both houses of Congress for the first time in forty years. Committed to reducing the cost and size of government, the Republican leadership eliminated all legislative service organizations, including the women's caucus. Such organizations could still exist, but they were to become congressional member organizations and would no longer receive public funding to pay for office space and staff. As a result, the bipartisan cochairs of the organization now take on the responsibilities of the caucus in addition to their regular duties as members of the House.

Most (but not all) women in the House are members; the legislative priorities that became law include (1) stronger child care funding and child support provisions as part of welfare reform in 1996; (2) increased spending for and eventual reauthorization of the Violence Against Women Act programs; (3) contraceptive coverage for women participating in the Federal Employee Health Benefits Program; (4) Medicaid coverage for low-income women diagnosed with breast cancer; and (5) the reinforcement of stalking, sex offender, and date rape laws, as well as many other pieces of legislation dealing with women's issues. With one exception during the 1990s, the bipartisan membership of the caucus has agreed to take a neutral stand on the issue of abortion to keep the organization more inclusive. The caucus also continues to pursue alliances with women senators, as well as with the House and Senate leadership in both parties, other caucuses, and the White House. Although more than two hundred caucuses have existed in the House in recent years to focus on a variety of policy issues, the Congressional Caucus for Women's Issues (along with the Congressional Black Caucus) has remained one of the most resilient and successful. In order for the caucus to continue to succeed, it must "celebrate its diversity while channeling the tremendous energy and talent of the growing membership into concrete legislative action."[22]

■ Women in State Legislatures

Historically, state legislatures have presented important political opportunities for women; it has been at the state level that women

Congressional Leadership:
One More Glass Ceiling Broken

In 1925, Representative Mae Ella Nolan (R-CA) became the first woman to chair a congressional committee when, during the 68th Congress, she chaired the Committee on Expenditures in the Post Office Department. Nearly eight decades later, another representative from California, Democrat Nancy Pelosi, became the highest-ranking woman to ever hold a leadership position when her Democratic colleagues supported her as the House minority leader in 2003. Four years later, Pelosi would make history again when she became speaker of the House at the start of the 110th Congress in 2007. Although more women than ever before are now serving in Congress, the top leadership positions have remained an important and elusive glass ceiling. Pelosi served as the Democratic whip, and then–Democratic minority leader, prior to her ascension, yet she remains the only woman to ever hold such a leadership position in either house of Congress.

Why are leadership posts so important within Congress? As a political institution, Congress is dominated by party politics. And the US Constitution helps to maintain our two-party system of government with single-member congressional districts. Thus, a candidate needs a simple majority (or plurality if more than two candidates are on the ballot) to win a congressional seat and represent all citizens within the district. The difficulty in a third-party candidate's winning the majority of votes in a congressional district helps to preserve the two-party system. As a result, the two major parties—Democrats and Republicans—control the rules that govern the policymaking process within Congress.

In the House of Representatives, the speaker comes from the majority party. The speaker refers bills to committees, appoints members to special committees, and grants members the right to speak during debates. After the speaker, the top leadership posts in the House include the majority leader and whip and the minority leader and whip. The party leaders and whips try to organize their members to support or oppose legislative proposals. Whips are usually selected from among the most experienced members of the House. Majority party members also chair and hold a majority of seats on both the House and Senate standing committees and subcommittees. The Senate is similar with regard to majority and minority leaders and whips, but it does not have a speaker.

continues

Congressional Leadership *continued*

Pelosi did not seek elective office until her five children were mostly grown; she has been in the House of Representatives since 1987, representing California's 8th District (which includes most of San Francisco). Her father, Thomas J. D'Alesandro, Jr., was a former congressman and mayor of Baltimore. Since first taking over the position of House minority leader in 2003, followed by speaker in 2007, Pelosi has earned a reputation as a pragmatic leader who is not afraid to speak her mind in public. Throughout her congressional career, she has also been known as a top Democratic fund-raiser and policy strategist. However, the Democrats' choice of Pelosi for minority leader in 2003 was questioned by many political commentators, even those sympathetic to the party's policy positions, due to her image as a San Francisco liberal. She took over the job from Richard Gephardt, a more centrist Democrat from Missouri, but her voting record seems to be in line with a majority of House Democrats, even if it does not represent the views of mainstream Democratic voters nationwide.[23] While moderate Democrats prefer the leadership style of Gephardt, who was always careful not to offend anyone with his positions, liberals like Pelosi's inclination to come out swinging. For instance, in May 2004, frustrated by the Bush administration's policies on the war in Iraq, she criticized President George W. Bush by saying, "I believe that the president's leadership and the actions taken in Iraq demonstrate an incompetence in terms of knowledge, judgment and experience."

In 2006, Pelosi was quite candid with the press about her intention to help the Democrats regain control of the House so that she could become the first woman speaker. Achieving that historic feat with Democrats in the majority in both houses of Congress, Pelosi announced her plan to push through major items on the Democratic policy agenda within the "first hundred hours" of the 110th Congress. Nearly all of the items on the legislative plan were passed, including an increase in the federal minimum wage, a reduction in student loan interest rates, new rules for Medicare prescription drug costs, increased funding for stem cell research, stricter rules for lobbyists, "pay-as-you-go" spending to reduce the national deficit, an end to tax subsidies for oil companies, and an increase in port security (as recommended by the 9/11 Commission). In addition, Pelosi continued to be an outspoken critic of many of the Bush administration's policies, particularly

continues

Congressional Leadership *continued*

the war in Iraq. However, she disappointed many liberals in the Democratic Party when she announced, after becoming speaker, that impeachment proceedings would not be pursued against President George W. Bush or Vice President Dick Cheney for their decision to invade Iraq in 2003. In 2008, Pelosi's support of Barack Obama helped to solidify the presidential candidate's support among Democratic voters; she campaigned tirelessly as well to increase the Democratic majority in the House. In 2009, her outspoken style of leadership continued as she publicly charged the CIA with having misled Congress with respect to torture and other aspects of the Bush administration's war on terror since 2001.

Pelosi, who broke an important congressional glass ceiling as the first woman to lead her party, has been called an "elegant and energetic" politician with "the kind of star quality that many say makes them again excited to be Democrats. Young women come to the Capitol to have their picture taken in front of her office."[24] It may be too early in her tenure as speaker to determine if her gender makes a difference in terms of the legislative agenda or the day-to-day, bipartisan functioning of the House, and it is important to remember that the institutional limitations, traditions, and procedures within the House, as well as standard party politics, may leave little room for change based on gendered leadership. However, as speaker of the House and second in line for succession to the presidency (after the vice president), Pelosi is the highest-ranking woman politician in the history of the United States.

have come closest to achieving representational parity with men. Women began to make substantial progress during the 1970s in getting elected to state legislatures, and that progress continued through the 1990s. When serving in leadership positions in state legislatures, women tend to differ from their male colleagues in important ways, namely that they "approach politics with an understanding and skills that have been shaped by family, community, volunteerism, and education. . . . Women are older, defer political careers until past their primary years of childrearing and family responsibilities, and hone their leadership ability in the classroom and community center rather than in the boardroom and locker room."[25] Women also engage in different legislative activities than men, spending more time on constituent concerns, building coalitions both within and across party lines, and studying proposed legislation; thus "women appear to be better team players with the legislature than are men." However, women legislators spend equal amounts of time as men on traditional legislative activities such as campaigning, fund-raising, seeking pork-barrel legislation (which brings state funds home to their district), and introducing new legislation.[26] One study also suggests that there is a "professionalization gap," meaning that women are "more likely than men to perceive their legislative careers as a full-time rather than a part-time job."[27]

Research has also shown that, in general, women legislators at the state level serve as "agents of policy-related change" in representing economically disadvantaged constitutents, reprioritizing state expenditures, and conducting business in public rather than in the backrooms of old. Women legislators have also given more priority than their male colleagues to legislation dealing with health care, welfare issues concerning family and children, and policies to help other women.[28] They are more liberal across the board than their male colleagues regardless of party affiliation.[29] As the number of women in state legislatures has grown, and as women legislators have worked together through political caucuses, they have been able to move issues of greatest concern to women (such as family leave, domestic violence, and comparable worth) into the legislative mainstream of state policy agendas.[30]

State legislatures are important to women in politics for several reasons. First, they are an important entry point for women who seek higher political office. Second, the rate of gains for women at the state level directly impacts the percentage of women serving in Congress and in other executive branch positions. And third, state legislatures decide many of the policy issues that have historically been of direct concern to women (such as education, health care, and workplace policies).[31] Like their counterparts in Congress, many women in state legislatures pay considerable attention to domestic and women's issues; yet as a group, their policy choices are diverse, and they do not represent a voting bloc committed to women's issues alone.[32] Historically, legislative sessions have been scheduled to accommodate the schedules and economic responsibilities of men, for instance the cycles of planting, growing, and harvesting crops when the nation had a primarily agricultural economy. Based on that tradition, the legislative schedule can still create a burden for women, who "experience the schedule of legislative life differently. . . . Even in contemporary times, as women participate in larger numbers in the paid labor force, the weight of household obligations continues to discourage women from legislative service. Women legislators are significantly more likely to serve in districts that are closer to the state capital, commuting daily to balance public and private duties."[33]

The first women to serve as state legislators were elected prior to the turn of the twentieth century—namely, Clara Cressingham, Carrie C. Holly, and Frances Klock, who were elected to the Colorado House of Representatives in 1894. Two years later, in 1896, Martha Hughes Cannon was elected to the Utah State Senate, becoming the first woman state senator. More than a century later, many more women had followed in the paths of these early women politicians. According to the Center for American Women and Politics, in 2009, 1,792 (24.3 percent) of the 7,382 state legislators in the United States were women, holding 437 (22.2 percent) of the 1,971 state senate seats and 1,355 (25 percent) of the 5,411 state house or assembly seats. Since 1971, the number of women serving in state legislatures has increased fivefold. Of the women state legislators serving in 2009, nearly one-fifth (19.5 percent) were women of color. [34]

In the last few years, however, women's electoral progress has slowed a bit in all three branches of state government—legislative, executive, and judicial—and the number of women in elective state office has leveled off nationwide. Not many clear patterns exist across states to explain this development. However, two trends do emerge. One is that a majority of women legislators are Democrats; Democratic women outnumber Republican women in state legislatures in spite of a nationwide voting trend from the mid-1990s until 2008 favoring Republicans. Of all women state senators, 70.2 percent are Democrats; of all women state representatives, 70.8 are Democrats. The other is that southern states lag behind other states in electing women to state legislatures. Table 5.3 shows that many of the states with the smallest percentage of women legislators are found in the South. In fact, only one southern state—Florida—has remained competitive with other top-ranked states in electing women to state legislative office.[35]

In the 1990s, women began to make substantial progress in

Table 5.3 Women in State Legislatures, 2009

State	No. of Women/ Total	Percentage
Alabama	17/140	12.1
Alaska	12/60	20.0
Arizona	28/90	31.1
Arkansas	32/135	23.7
California	33/120	27.5
Colorado	39/100	39.0
Connecticut	59/187	31.6
Delaware	15/62	24.2
Florida	38/160	23.8
Georgia	44/236	18.6
Hawaii	25/76	32.9
Idaho	26/105	24.8
Illinois	49/177	27.7
Indiana	33/150	22.0
Iowa	34/150	22.7
Kansas	47/165	28.5
Kentucky	21/138	15.2
Louisiana	22/144	15.3
Maine	54/186	29.0
Maryland	59/188	31.4
Massachusetts	52/200	26.0
Michigan	37/148	25.0
Minnesota	70/201	34.8
Mississippi	25/174	14.4
Missouri	41/197	20.8
Montana	39/150	26.0
Nebraska	10/49	20.4
Nevada	20/63	31.7
New Hampshire	158/424	37.3
New Jersey	37/120	30.8
New Mexico	34/112	30.4
New York	52/212	24.5
North Carolina	43/170	25.3
North Dakota	22/141	15.6
Ohio	28/132	21.3
Oklahoma	17/149	11.4
Oregon	25/90	27.8
Pennsylvania	37/253	14.6
Rhode Island	25/113	22.1
South Carolina	17/170	10.0
South Dakota	20/105	19.0
Tennessee	24/132	18.2
Texas	42/181	23.8
Utah	23/104	22.1
Vermont	67/180	37.2
Virginia	24/140	17.1
Washington	48/147	32.0
West Virginia	22/134	16.4
Wisconsin	29/132	22.0
Wyoming	16/90	17.8
Total	1,792/7,382	24.3

Source: Center for American Women and Politics, Rutgers, The State University of New Jersey.

holding state legislative leadership positions. By 2009, twenty-seven women (thirteen Democrats and fourteen Republicans) in sixteen states had served as speakers, and nineteen women (eleven Democrats and eight Republicans) in twelve states had served as senate presidents. When all leadership positions, not just the top posts, are considered, the percentages are even higher. Through 2007, a total of fifty-nine (17.6 percent) of all leadership positions in state legislatures were held by women, and women also chaired a total of 403 (22.6 percent) standing committees in state legislatures.[36] It is clear that when more women are elected to state legislatures, more women assume positions of state leadership, either as party leaders or committee chairs.[37] A "feminization" of state legislative leadership has also occurred. Not only has the increased number of women legislators led to more women holding leadership positions, but a more "feminine" leadership style that emphasizes consensus and compromise has emerged among both women *and* men in leadership positions.[38] Women have also capitalized on legislative power by holding committee chairs, which emphasizes "getting the job done" in terms of passing legislation as opposed to positional authority through a higher leadership position such as the House (or Assembly) or Senate leader; in these positions, women committee chairs "appear to be more comfortable developing their influence through group efforts aimed at solving a problem or achieving a desired outcome."[39]

Conclusion

Considering the progress made to date, an increase in the number of women legislators at both the state and national level seems inevitable. Women benefit the political process by offering "a greater diversity of ideas and experiences that fuel definition of problems and the creation of solutions."[40] In order for the number of women serving in legislatures at both the state and national level to continue to increase, strong recruitment efforts must be undertaken. All political candidates need an adequate amount of money as well as support from relevant interest groups and party leadership to be competitive in a campaign. Incumbent women also need to identify and mentor other women to run for similar office.[41]

Research conducted on both Congress and state legislatures has shown that women do make a difference in policy outcomes, particularly those that directly affect women. However, women have yet to have a significant impact on day-to-day legislative norms and practices. Nonetheless, women, "though few in number and relatively new to positions of institutional power, are transforming our understanding of the nature of representation and are dramatically reshaping the agenda and representation of interests in Congress."[42] The same trend has emerged at the state level, where women continue to gain access to the legislative process in their quest to be equal participants in policymaking at all levels of government.

■ Study/Discussion Questions

1. Why is integrative/transformational leadership more effective in legislatures, and how might women legislators benefit from this strategy?

2. Why didn't suffrage immediately lead to an increase of women in political office?

3. How does the Congressional Caucus for Women's Issues impact the legislative agenda in Congress?

4. Why are leadership positions in Congress so important? How might women impact policymaking by holding these positions?

5. Why are state legislatures such important venues for women's issues? How do they benefit women seeking a political career?

■ Online Resources

Speaker of the House Nancy Pelosi. http://speaker.house.gov.
US House of Representatives. http://www.house.gov.
US Senate. http://www.senate.gov.
Women in Congress. http://womenincongress.house.gov.
Women's Policy, Inc., The Unique Source of Information on Women's Issues in Congress. http://www.womenspolicy .org.

■ Notes

1. Rosenthal, *When Women Lead*, 7.
2. Ibid., 162.
3. Ibid., 21–22.
4. Ibid., 160.
5. Rosenthal, "Women Leading Legislatures," 197–212.
6. See Center for American Women and Politics, "Fast Facts: Congress"; see also Wilson, *Closing the Leadership Gap*, 4.
7. Schroeder, "Running for Our Lives," 28-31.
8. Ibid., 33.
9. Quoted in Whitney, *Nine and Counting*, 117–118.
10. Ibid., 47–48.
11. Thomas, *How Women Legislate*, 153.
12. Center for American Women and Politics, "Women of Color in Elective Office 2009." Eagleton Institute of Politics, Rutgers, The State University of New Jersey, available at http://www.cawp.rutgers.edu/fast_facts/levels_of_office/documents/color.pdf.
13. Thomas, *How Women Legislate*, 100.
14. Carroll, "Representing Women," 66.
15. US House of Representatives, "Biography of Congresswoman Loretta Sanchez."http://www.lorettasanchez.house.gov/index.php?option=com_content&view=article&id=18&Itemid=53.
16. "The Changing Face of Orange County."
17. Rodriguez, "A Modern-Day Helen of Troy?"
18. Hearn, "Sanchez Accuses Democrat of Calling Her a 'Whore.'"
19. Swers and Larson, "Women in Congress," 110–128.
20. Quoted in Whitney, *Nine and Counting*, 129–130.
21. Whitney, *Nine and Counting*, 3.
22. Hall, "The Congressional Caucus for Women's Issues at 25," 348.
23. Suellentrop, "The Leader the House Democrats Deserve."
24. Stolberg, "A Nation at War," B13.
25. Rosenthal, *When Women Lead*, 161.
26. Carey, Niemi, and Powell, "Are Women Legislators Different?" 100–101.
27. Epstein, Niemi, and Powell, "Do Women and Men State Legislators Differ?" 94–109.
28. Carroll, "Representing Women," 17–18.
29. Carey, Niemi, and Powell, "Are Women Legislators Different?" 101.
30. Thomas and Welch, "The Impact of Women in State Legislatures," 178.
31. Ford and Dolan, "Women State Legislators," 205.
32. Ibid., 216.
33. Rosenthal, *When Women Lead*, 13–14.
34. Center for American Women and Politics, "Women in State Legislatures 2009."

35. Ibid. See also Carroll, "Women in State Government."

36. Center for American Women and Politics, "Women in State Legislatures 2009" and "Women State Legislators: Leadership Positions and Committee Chairs 2007."

37. Carroll, "Women in State Government."

38. Whicker and Jewell, "The Feminization of Leadership in State Legislatures," 174.

39. Rosenthal, "Getting Things Done," 186.

40. Thomas, *How Women Legislate*, 147.

41. Carroll, "Women in State Government."

42. Rosenthal, *Women Transforming Congress*, 11.

6

Women and
Executive Leadership

What would it be like if women ran the world?
■ Sally Helgesen, author of *The Female Advantage:*
Women's Ways of Leadership

Will America ever elect a woman president? This has become a
popular question and has been the topic of several books, academic conferences, public opinion polls, and lectures in women and
politics courses on college campuses across the country. Yet
despite all the attention paid to the possibility and the opinion of
experts that it is not a matter of *if* but *when*, there has been only
one serious female presidential contender to date: Hillary
Rodham Clinton. Prior to Clinton's run for the White House in
2008, Patricia Schroeder in 1988, Elizabeth Dole in 2000, and
Carol Moseley Braun in 2004 each had short-lived presidential
campaigns. All four women share accomplished political careers:
Clinton is a former first lady and had been a US senator representing New York for six years when she announced her campaign
in 2007; Schroeder represented Colorado in the House for twenty-four years; Dole, a former US senator from North Carolina,
had served as both secretary of transportation and secretary of
labor; and Moseley Braun was the first black woman ever to serve
in the US Senate, representing Illinois; she was also the US
ambassador to New Zealand during the Clinton administration.
Unlike Clinton, however, Schroeder, Dole, and Moseley Braun
did not survive the presidential campaign process long enough to
have a single vote cast in their favor in a presidential primary or

caucus. For Clinton's part, though she fell short of capturing the Democratic nomination, her historic win in the New Hampshire primary in January 2008 signaled that a new era of presidential politics had begun.[1]

Although women have made great strides in achieving legislative office, as discussed in Chapter 5, there still seems to be a dearth of women executive leaders in government, business, and other institutions of US society. From the top spot in the Oval Office to governor's mansions, city halls, and corporate boardrooms across the country, executive leadership positions are still dominated by men. This chapter will discuss executive political leadership and the barriers faced by women politicians in gaining access to these seats of power. First, we will look at how women in the corporate world have defined successful leadership to determine if there are any lessons to be learned for women seeking political executive positions. Then we will consider the potential of electing a woman president and vice president, as well as the impact of women in other prominent executive positions—cabinet members and other White House staff positions, first ladies, state governors, and mayors.

■ Executive Leadership from a Woman's Perspective

The job of the US president is often compared to that of a chief executive officer (CEO) of a large corporation. Unlike legislators, who by the very nature of their position must cooperate on some level with colleagues, a president has no counterpart and is ultimately responsible for making executive decisions. Several politicians have sought either the presidency or the position of state governor based on their successful careers as corporate executives. Business executives often reason that if they can run a major corporation, they can run a government bureaucracy. For example, in 1992, H. Ross Perot received 19 percent of the popular vote in the presidential election due to his emphasis on fiscal responsibility, a trait he attributed to his long career as a leader in the corporate world. Similarly, former Massachusetts governor Mitt Romney has long equated his many years as a corporate executive with the experience necessary to be a successful executive leader in government; Romney won eleven Republican primaries and caucuses in the 2008 presidential campaign (before losing the nomination to John McCain) in part by touting his business credentials.

Whether or not a successful CEO could also effectively run the executive branch of the federal government remains to be seen. However, the political and business sectors share traditionally masculine structures, environments, and cultures. Women have been slow to make substantial gains in either, if for no other reason than that insufficient time has passed since the women's movement of the late 1960s began to break down the social and cultural barriers keeping women from executive positions. Women need both time and credentials to work their way up into business and political leadership positions. Executive positions of power have always been male dominated; thus, gender plays an important role in determining successful leadership traits. A woman "cannot enter a post previously held by a male and be entirely interchangeable with him—in meaning at least."[2]

How do women business executives fare in a male-dominated arena, and are there instructive comparisons for women governors or a future woman president? Much has now been written about how women's leadership styles in the business world—based on building inclusive relationships—have been better for business than the traditional hierarchical system. Management literature has embraced the notion of unique female leadership qualities, as well as emotional intelligence (the ability to recognize and control one's emotions).[3] Much has also been written about how female leadership characteristics and principles—such as communication, personal relationships, community building, and ignoring the rigid hierarchy of most corporations—provide an important advantage to women in the corporate world.[4] However, many of these same women fear that acknowledging that a difference exists between male and female leadership traits will be the same as admitting inequality. As a result, women are often "wedged into stereotypes, often acting against female values, trying to fit the male definition of leadership."[5]

The old paradigm of leadership, defined as masculine within a hierarchical, command-and-control structure, shows an opposition to change. This style of leadership is defined by individual (as opposed to group) efforts and an inclination toward indirect communication that trickles down through the organization's vertical structure.[6] However, many successful women in business have

adopted a new paradigm of leadership. Women used to try to succeed in managerial positions by acting more like men, dressing in
suits and using a structured, top-down approach that limited their
access to colleagues and customers—a "command-and-control
style long associated with the masculine mind-set." But by the
mid- to late 1990s, female corporate executives like Meg
Whitman of eBay, Inc., and Marcy Carsey of the Carsey-Werner
Company had developed effective strategies for growing their
businesses on their terms. These new leaders were "noted for
their abilities to blend feminine qualities of leadership with classic
male traits to run their companies successfully and become some
of the most powerful women in American business."[7]

Esther Wachs Book, author of *Why the Best Man for the Job Is
a Woman*, states that women who adopt the new paradigm of leadership succeed for three main reasons: (1) self-assurance compels
them to stay motivated and to take risks; (2) an emphasis on cus-
tomer service helps them anticipate market changes; and (3) using
their "feminine" traits to their advantage—empathy, collaboration, and cooperation—allow them to negotiate with their own
leadership styles. As a result, acknowledging differences between
men and women and their leadership styles makes more
approaches available. The book identifies seven key characteristics
of new paradigm leadership: (1) an ability to sell the vision, (2) a
willingness to reinvent the rules, (3) a laser focus on achievement,
(4) an emphasis on high touch in an era of high tech, (5) a knack
for turning challenge into opportunity, (6) an obsession with cus-
tomer preferences, and (7) courage under fire.[8]

Like women in politics, women in business careers also face
barriers in reaching the top of the corporate ladder. Childrearing
and other family responsibilities top the list, along with the per-
petuation of the stereotype that women are not tough, aggressive,
or ambitious enough to make it to the corner office. Studies have
also shown that men are often reluctant to place women in positions of power over others in work settings.[9] Perhaps one of the
most notable women CEOs is Carleton S. "Carly" Fiorina of
Hewlett-Packard, who exhibited a leadership style during her six
years (1999–2005) at the helm of the computer giant that even
other women corporate officers admit makes her a tough act to
follow. Fiorina gained her position not by promoting her difference as a woman and employing the new paradigm of leadership

but by following the more traditional, power-driven male path. Most women in business have not followed Fiorina's model. At the time of this writing in 2009, women hold only a small percentage of the top-level jobs in major US companies, and only fifteen, although more than ever before, are CEOs of Fortune 500 companies.[10] To many observers, this suggests that "unbridled ambition is less acceptable in women than in men."[11] However, Fiorina's public ouster from HP in early 2005 may suggest that following the new paradigm may be the better option for women in corporate America.

According to Marie Wilson, founder of the White House Project (a nonpartisan organization dedicated to placing more women in top government and business leadership positions), "Ambition in men is an expectation and a virtue. In women, it can be a kiss of death, guaranteeing isolation, ending relationships (personal and professional), pushing entire families into therapy, and making even the most self-assured CEO wonder what she was thinking."[12] Although Wilson views women today as equal competitors with men in terms of education, experience, and skill, she claims success is based more on how hard a person chooses to compete rather than gender discrimination, and "the folks who tend to compete the hardest are generally the stereotypically manly men." Some studies and news media reports have suggested that women would be happier if they give up positions of power in return for more quality time in their lives for family, friends, and other non-business pursuits.[13] In addition, other studies suggest that women are less willing than men to make family sacrifices in order to climb the corporate ladder. Nonetheless, women are often conflicted about such decisions, believing that they will somehow fail other women in their profession if they choose family over career. But many of those reports have been challenged as not being representative of the larger population of women, evidence that suggests women in business are just as competitive as men and equally aspire to be a CEO, regardless of whether or not they have children and family responsibilities.[14] In addition, women corporate executives are still viewed as anomalies, just as many women politicians are, and an inordinate amount of media attention is paid to women CEOs who leave their positions, particularly if they are fired (even though CEOs are fired fairly regularly in the business world).[15]

■ **Electing a Woman President**

The executive branch is perhaps the most masculine of the three
branches of government, due mostly to its hierarchical structure,
unity of command, and the ability for a president to act decisively
when the need arises. The presidency also "operates on the great
man model of leadership," leaving women defined as the "other"
in the executive branch.[16] Creating a strong image of presidential
leadership in the minds of citizens is essential for any politician
who aspires to the Oval Office. Strong leadership has historically
been defined as an attempt to exert one's will over a particular situation, a societal view that "has been conditioned by the interpretation of American history as written." This affects how the public
will view all aspiring leaders, particularly women.[17] Relatedly,
many citizens value "presidential machismo," which is the image
desired by many Americans to have their president exhibit tough
and aggressive behavior on the international stage. Even though
the unilateral actions of a president to wage war or carry out other
military actions may run "counter to aspects of democratic theory
of governance," public opinion polls routinely show that
Americans admire this type of behavior by presidents, forming
"the basis of a cult that often elevates presidents, primarily those
regarded as strong and who waged successful wars, to the status of
heroes."[18]

Once in office, presidents must remember that their job, by
constitutional design, is one of both shared and limited powers. A
paradox exists in that Americans expect great things from their
president, but "the resources at the disposal of the president are
limited and the system in which a president operates can easily
frustrate efforts at presidential leadership."[19] As such, presidents
must maximize their opportunities to gain influence and achieve
success with their policy agendas, in dealing with Congress, and
certainly in the eyes of the US public in determining job approval.
Other factors must also be considered if presidents are to maximize their leadership potential, including effectiveness as a public
communicator, organizational capacity (staffing and leadership
skills within the White House), cognitive style (intellectual
curiosity coupled with either attention to detail or abstract thinking skills), and emotional intelligence.[20] Assuming that women
tend to exhibit a leadership style based on cooperation, compro-

mise, and emotional intelligence, we can conclude that a woman president would be no more constrained in this area than her male counterpart and might even enjoy a strategic advantage.[21]

That assumes, however, that women presidential contenders can overcome the many barriers that exist. Aside from the constitutional requirements for the office of the presidency—at least thirty-five years of age, natural-born citizenship, and fourteen years of residency—no formal criteria exist for presidential candidates. However, several informal qualifications have historically limited the pool of potential nominees, with factors such as religion, race, and gender shrinking the pool of viable candidates for both president and vice president to include almost exclusively Protestant white males.[22] Obviously, the election of Barack Obama in 2008 broke a significant barrier in terms of race, but the effect his election will have on the campaigns of presidential candidates of color in the future remains to be seen. As for religion, John F. Kennedy, a Catholic, remains the only non-Protestant to hold the office of the presidency, and Joseph Lieberman remains the only Jewish candidate for president or vice president after his nomination as Al Gore's running mate in 2000. The health and age of candidates, as well as their family ties and personal relationships (particularly their marital status and record on fidelity) are also important.[23]

The character, personality, and style of presidential candidates are crucial to voters. Although party affiliation and policy preferences are still an important factor among voters, the decline of partisan loyalty and the desire for party nominees to appeal to moderate, middle-of-the-road voters during most general election campaigns in recent decades has placed more emphasis on the candidate as an individual. During the television age, political news reporting has become more cynical, sensationalized, and hypercritical, which has led to an increased focus on the "cult of personality" during presidential campaigns.[24] Whereas "character" may be a broadly defined term, Americans today look for, among other things, honesty, integrity, intelligence, strong communication skills, flexibility, compassion, open-mindedness, and a commitment to both the public good and the democratic process in their presidential candidates.[25] For women candidates, it is even more important to develop an effective communication strategy to combat negative stereotypes in the news media (as discussed in

Chapter 3) and emphasize their "perceived image and issue strengths—honesty and trustworthiness and dealing with social concerns—as well as [establishing their] credibility as tough and decisive leader[s] able to handle such issues as crime, foreign policy, and the economy."[26] Showing strength and experience in the foreign policy arena also remains important for women presidential candidates in the post-9/11 era.

Where, then, do Americans find presidential and vice presidential candidates? A short list of presidential candidates—put together in part by the news media through speculation based on the behavior and travel patterns of notable politicians (for example, who is traveling to Iowa and New Hampshire, or speaking at high-profile party events)—usually consists of notable members of Congress, governors from larger states, and former or current vice presidents. This "on-deck circle" consists of roughly thirty to forty individuals in any given presidential election year, and can include governors, prominent US senators, a few members of the House of Representatives, and a handful of recent governors or vice presidents who have remained prominent in the news media.[27] Given that four of the last six presidents were former governors, this type of political experience tends to elevate many candidates in the eyes of the news media. Although serving as a state governor is certainly not the only path to the White House, the dearth of women who have executive experience—either in politics or business—parallels their relative absence from the presidential short list. In addition, although women senators enjoy high national profiles, the US Senate is not a traditional place to look for presidential candidates. Barack Obama became the first president elected directly from the Senate since John F. Kennedy in 1960, and only the third in US history (the first being Warren Harding in 1920). Lack of congressional leadership also tends to keep women off the presidential short list; despite the historic speakership of Nancy Pelosi, she remains the only woman from either political party to ever hold a leadership position in the Congress.

Other keys to early success in a presidential campaign include name recognition in the news media, support among party elites, access to money (either personal wealth or strong fund-raising capabilities), and time to both campaign and fund-raise. In recent years, holding the office of the vice presidency or being a governor of a large state has elevated the public status of several presidential hopefuls. The Washington insider versus outsider phenomenon has also emerged; four of the last six presidents were previous state governors. The image of "master politician" with political experience and a substantive policy record, once necessary to run for the White House, has given way to the image of the Washington outsider, which requires strong speaking skills, an emphasis on anti-Washington rhetoric, and broad public appeal outside the beltway.[28] This outsider strategy proved successful for Governors Jimmy Carter of Georgia, Ronald Reagan of California, Bill Clinton of Arkansas, and George W. Bush of Texas—and even helped Barack Obama, who had only been in the US Senate since 2005.

Given all the requirements for viable presidential candidates, it should be obvious why no woman has yet been elected president—and why so few have even decided to run in the first place. The most glaring problem is that so few women hold the appropriate leadership positions within our government that allow them access to the "on-deck circle." There are several reasons for this, including the traditional view that men should hold public leadership roles while women should remain at home tending to domestic responsibilities and childrearing; a political system that is biased in favor of incumbents; the dearth of female role models for younger women who might aspire to political careers; the fact that women are less likely to be recruited to run for the presidency; and finally the double burden of work and family responsibilities that leads many professional women to postpone running for office until much later in life than men.[29] In addition, research has shown that the candidate emergence phase of a campaign—moving from a potential to an actual candidate—represents one of the biggest hurdles for women to overcome, particularly in seeking the presidency. The gender gap in political ambition is attributed to the fact that women are significantly less likely than men to receive encouragement (whether from a current or former politician or from a financial supporter) to run for office or to deem themselves qualified to run for office.[30]

With so much attention focused on electing a woman president, it is important to remember that the election of the first woman vice president would also be a significant breakthrough, as fourteen vice presidents have gone on to become president, either by succession following the death or resignation of an elected president or by election in their own right. Balancing the ticket is usually the goal of the nominee and his party in choosing a running mate according to ideology, geography, experience, insider/outsider status (for instance, a vice president who is a Washington insider may strengthen congressional relationships for an outsider president), healing a breach within the party, and whether or not the running mate hails from an electorally rich state. Today's vice presidential nominees "must possess some desirable qualities the presidential nominee lacks and must be acceptable to the presidential nominee . . . [although there is] little evidence to suggest that vice presidents add greatly to or detract severely from the popularity of presidential candidates with the voters."[31] Since Geraldine Ferraro's historic bid for the vice presidency as Democrat Walter Mondale's running mate in 1984, only one other woman has been nominated for vice president—Alaska governor Sarah Palin in 2008. When first announced as John McCain's running mate in September 2008, Palin catapulted to instant political celebrity as the first Republican woman to run for vice president. Yet for all of the excitement that her candidacy generated among the base of the Republican Party, she failed to garner the support of independent and crossover Democratic voters due to her social conservative views. In addition, despite the desire to elect a woman to the presidency or vice presidency, Democratic prochoice women who had supported Hillary Clinton in the primaries did not support Palin's candidacy. In addition, her political inexperience (she had been governor for fewer than two years) and lack of knowledge about major domestic and international issues caused many to question McCain's decision to choose her to be his running mate. Palin also became a flashpoint for feminism during the presidential campaign, fueling discussions about working mothers and family responsibilities as well as the roles of both liberal and conservative women in politics. Much attention was also focused on appearance and whether or not Palin was too attractive to be taken seriously as a national candidate. Regardless of one's opinion of Palin, her vice presidential candidacy did make history and expanded the diversity of women and their ideologies, perspectives, and personal histories on the national stage.

Despite the many barriers for a woman to be elected president, public opinion suggests continued support for electing a woman president, at least in theory. The gender, education, and political ideology of the respondents in the polls about electing a woman president seem to be the most prominent factors that shape public opinion, followed by age, race, and party identification.[32] Yet potential women presidential and vice presidential candidates are not always portrayed as authoritative in the press. Much like Ferraro in 1984, Elizabeth Dole "was covered more as a novelty than a serious candidate" in 1999, as the media took what the White House Project calls the "hair, hemlines, and husbands" approach to coverage.[33] Other studies have shown this trend, making gender a significant, and not always positive, label in news media coverage for women candidates.[34] However, that began to change somewhat following the 2004 presidential election with the anticipation of Hillary Rodham Clinton's presidential campaign. One of the most popular media narratives of the 2008 election revolved around the possibility of electing not just any female president but Clinton in particular. Clinton, along with Secretary of State Condoleezza Rice, were two of the most talked-about potential candidates leading up to the 2008 presidential election; both women had been at the top of public opinion polls for who voters would like to see running for president. By the end of 2006, most news organizations had all but given the Democratic nomination to Clinton, regularly labeling her the clear Democratic frontrunner (although the potential candidacy of Senator Barack Obama began to capture much media attention by the end of 2007 as well). The news media seemed to love the story of Hillary running for president (she was routinely referred to as simply "Hillary" by the news media). Surveys indicated that Americans would overwhelmingly support a woman candidate for president; in three separate polls in early 2006, a large majority of respondents said they would vote for a woman for president. A CBS News poll found that 92 percent of respondents said they would vote for a qualified woman, whereas a Hearst/Siena College Research Institute poll found that 79 percent of respondents were willing to vote for a woman, and 69 percent of respondents in the California Field Poll stated that the country was ready for a woman president.[35]

Yet, for all the excitement over Clinton's campaign, she would fall short of capturing the Democratic nomination in what was considered an epic political battle with Barack Obama. Clinton's chances of winning the nomination were never as strong as early media predictions suggested; despite her name recognition and star power among the US electorate and her presumed ability to raise large sums of campaign contributions, Clinton entered the presidential contest with high negatives among a large percentage of voters. Numerous other factors contributed to Clinton's failure to capture the Democratic nomination; among them were the lack of a consistent message (she both portrayed herself as the most experienced candidate and claimed that, as a woman, she would bring change to Washington), the lack of a fifty-state strategy (the Clinton campaign focused on the large states while the Obama campaign competed for every delegate in every state during the primaries), and the inability to compete with Obama in terms of fund-raising and the "ground game" (grassroots organizers and local volunteers who provide voter education, voter registration, and voter turnout). In addition, the Clinton campaign had been wracked with personality disputes and mismanagement that led to its "epic meltdown," as it "was not prepared for a lengthy fight; it had an insufficient delegate operation; it squandered vast sums of money; and the candidate herself evinced a paralyzing schizophrenia—one day a shots-'n'-beers brawler, the next a Hallmark Channel mom. Through it all, her staff feuded and bickered, while her husband distracted."[36] Despite Clinton's insistence that she had the executive and managerial competence to serve effectively as president, her campaign was poorly managed and the infighting often undermined its ability to execute the strategies that it had developed.

In the final analysis, was the Clinton campaign a trailblazing effort that paved the way for a future woman presidential candidate, or simply a campaign by a woman who was uniquely situated to run for president (due in part to her status as a former first lady) in a way that no other woman politician could match? The first woman president, whenever elected, will break through the ultimate glass ceiling in US politics. There has long been an assumption that a viable woman presidential candidate (that is, a candidate who could legitimately compete in primaries and caucuses and have a real chance at her party's nomination) would help to further break down barriers for woman candidates at all levels of government. Even though Clinton did not win her party's nomination, her campaign serves as an important milestone for women

Women and the Race for the White House:
The Contenders

The first female candidate for president dates back to 1872, when Victoria Woodhull, a stockbroker, publisher, and protégé of Cornelius Vanderbilt, ran for president on the Equal Rights Party ticket. She was followed on the same ticket in 1884 and 1888 by Belva Lockwood, the first woman admitted to practice law before the US Supreme Court and an active participant in the women's suffrage movement. Eight decades would pass before the next woman would officially seek the presidency. Senator Margaret Chase Smith, a Maine Republican, dropped out of the race after placing fifth in the New Hampshire primary. Smith, who made history by becoming the first woman to serve in both houses of Congress (elected to the House of Representatives in 1940 to replace her dying husband, and elected to the Senate in 1948), was also nominated for the presidency by Vermont senator George Aiken at the Republican National Convention in 1964.

Shirley Chisholm, the first black woman to serve in Congress (a Democrat in the House of Representatives), ran for president in 1972. In doing so, Chisholm stunned friends and colleagues with her decision, yet used her candidacy in the Democratic primary to raise awareness on issues such as education and other social programs. Even though her name was placed on the ballot in twelve primary states, Chisholm never received more than seven percent of the vote in any of the primary contests.[37] Since then, and before Hillary Clinton in 2008, no woman in either major political party had sustained a presidential campaign long enough to have a vote cast in her favor in either the Iowa caucus or the New Hampshire primary. Patricia Schroeder seriously considered a run for the presidency in 1988 after Democratic frontrunner Gary Hart dropped out of the race in the spring of 1987. Her campaign, however, never made it out of the exploratory mode and officially ended in September 1987. Elizabeth Dole had a much stronger campaign organization going into the 2000 Republican primaries, yet when money and positive news coverage both eluded her in the fall of 1999, she too withdrew from the presidential race.

Unlike Schroeder and Dole, who both fared well enough in early public opinion polls to give their campaigns temporary credibility, Carol Moseley Braun was a long shot for the 2004 Democratic presidential nomination from the outset. Nonetheless, although she dropped out of the race in January 2004, prior to the

continues

Women and the Race for the White House *continued*

Iowa caucus, Moseley Braun made it onto a total of twenty primary ballots, more than any other woman, Democrat or Republican, ever had before. She also performed well in several televised debates as the only woman in a field of mostly white men and was credited with bringing a unique voice to the political discussion in the early days of the 2004 presidential race. She also had a major player in the women's rights movement as her campaign manager—Patricia Ireland, prominent feminist author and former president of the National Organization for Women. Moseley Braun's favorite line on the campaign trail illustrated why voters should take her candidacy seriously: "I'm the clearest alternative to George Bush. I don't look like him. I don't talk like him. I don't think like him. And I certainly don't act like him."[38]

Then, in 2008, Hillary Rodham Clinton made history. She became the first woman to win a presidential nominating contest (the New Hampshire primary in January 2008), which also resulted in earning delegates to the national convention.[39] In total, Clinton would win twenty-one primaries (Arizona, Arkansas, California, Florida, Indiana, Kentucky, Massachusetts, Michigan, New Hampshire, New Jersey, New Mexico, New York, Ohio, Pennsylvania, Puerto Rico, Rhode Island, South Dakota, Tennessee, Texas, Utah, and West Virginia) and one caucus (Nevada).[40] She earned 1,896 delegates out of 4,934 total, with 2,118 needed for the nomination, prior to the Democratic National Convention and amassed a total of 18,046,007 popular votes during the Democratic nomination process.[41] Clinton also helped to recruit new voters excited by the possibility of electing a woman president, and her candidacy proved that white, male, working-class voters in states such as Ohio and Pennsylvania would vote for a woman. Perhaps most important, after watching Clinton on the campaign trail for eighteen months, many Americans grew accustomed to seeing a woman candidate as a serious contender for the White House.

And how might future women presidential candidates fare? Following the 2008 campaign, the names of several prominent women politicians began to emerge as potential candidates in future elections, including Health and Human Services Secretary (and former Kansas governor) Kathleen Sebelius (D), former New Jersey governor and former head of the Environmental Protection Agency Christine Todd Whitman (R), Connecticut governor Jodi

continues

Women and the Race for the White House *continued*

Rell (R), Alaska senator Lisa Murkowski (R), and Florida congress-woman Debbie Wasserman Shultz (D). Canadian-born Michigan governor Jennifer Granholm is also mentioned as someone who would be on the short list for president were she a natural-born US citizen (she was born in Canada). Although many of her supporters still talk about a Clinton candidacy in 2016, Clinton's own comments about not running again (she told Fox News in October 2008 the chances were "probably close to zero") as well as her age (she would be 68 at the start of 2016), suggest that her chance of becoming president has probably passsed.

in US politics by achieving many "firsts" on the presidential campaign trail. Clinton's candidacy showed an unprecedented level of willingness among American voters to cast a ballot for the first woman president. In the long term, that is perhaps the most important legacy of Clinton's 2008 presidential campaign, as it leaves a solid achievement on which future women presidential candidates may build.

■ Women in the Executive Branch

Although no woman has yet served as president or vice president, women have taken an increasingly prominent role in other positions in the executive branch. Beginning in the 1960s and continuing through the 1970s, the link between the presidency and women—both in terms of appointments within the executive branch and in terms of policies relevant to women—became much stronger. During the 1980s, although Ronald Reagan appointed the first woman to the US Supreme Court, the number of overall appointments of women to positions within the administration declined. With George H.W. Bush's election in 1988, however, the numbers again increased, as did the amount of attention paid to women's issues.[42] The next two presidents, Bill Clinton and George W. Bush, appointed women to executive posts in record numbers, partly in recognition of the political importance of women voters and interest groups devoted to women's issues. This trend has continued with the Obama administration. Three avenues of influence for women within both the White House and the federal bureaucracy include presidential appointments to cabinet and other cabinet-level positions, posts within the White House as presidential advisers, and the unofficial yet sometimes powerful role of first lady.

The President's Cabinet

As we discussed in Chapter 1, women have held only forty-five cabinet or cabinet-level positions since the presidential cabinet was established in 1789. Frances Perkins became the first woman to serve in a cabinet when Franklin D. Roosevelt appointed her as secretary of labor. Madeleine Albright, who served as secretary of state during Bill Clinton's administration (1996–2001), became the highest-ranking woman to ever serve in the cabinet. The rank of cabinet offices is based on presidential succession as well as four "inner" cabinet positions that have been designated as such by presidency scholars due to the influence of the positions in national policymaking. The "inner" cabinets include the Departments of State, Justice, Defense, and Treasury. According to the Presidential Succession Act of 1947, cabinet members follow the vice president, speaker of the House of Representatives, and the president pro tempore of the Senate based on the date their offices were established. The first four cabinet members in line for succession are as follows: secretary of state, secretary of the treasury, secretary of defense, and the attorney general. However, Albright could not have served as president due to the constitutional requirement that presidents must be natural-born citizens, since she was born in Czechoslovakia.

During the mid-twentieth century, women cabinet appointments were usually viewed as tokenism. By the 1990s, however, the political climate had changed and public expectations had shifted, such that women cabinet appointments were seen as more routine. At the start of his administration in 2001, George W. Bush appointed three women to his cabinet—Elaine Chao (Department of Labor), Gale Norton (Department of the Interior), and Ann Veneman (Department of Agriculture)—and also appointed Christine Todd Whitman to a cabinet-level position as head of the Environmental Protection Agency. Bush sought to follow the example set by his predecessor, Bill Clinton, in appointing a cabinet that looked like the United States in terms of gender and ethnic diversity; a total of five women had served in cabinet positions during Clinton's two terms in office. Bush appointed two women to his second-term cabinet as well, including Condoleezza Rice, who moved from national security adviser to secretary of state (see Table 6.1). Similarly, Barack Obama appointed four women to his cabinet in 2009, including Hillary Rodham Clinton (Department of State), Hilda Solis (Department of Labor), Kathleen Sebelius (Department of Health and Human Services), and Janet Napolitano (Department of Homeland Security).

A president's nomination to a cabinet post is a signal of representation—the nominee reflects the president's agenda in that particular area of policy. Thus, the cabinet secretary represents the president's policy agenda to relevant constituents (voters, interest groups, Congress, state and local governments). Although many of the women who have served in the cabinet have done so in positions of influence over "women's issues," particularly in the Departments of Health and Human Services and Labor, women are increasingly being considered for a wider variety of posts within an administration. Even so, based on news media coverage and treatment during the confirmation process in the Senate, many of these women cabinet members are still viewed as token appointments. One recent study suggests "women have yet to be perceived as full participants in the cabinet, either as office holders or as constituents."[43]

White House Advisers

The size of the White House staff has grown dramatically during the past century. With the creation of the executive office of the president in 1937, a formal staff was put in place during Franklin Roosevelt's second term to help with the implementation of New Deal policies; ever since, the president's inner circle of advisers has grown in both numbers and influence. In the post–New Deal era, the role of the federal government in policymaking has only increased, and White House staffers now perform "integral and influential roles in both presidential policymaking and politics."[44]

Table 6.1 Women in the Cabinet, 1933 to Present

State
Madeleine Albright, 1996–2001 (Clinton)
Condoleezza Rice, 2005–2009 (Bush)
Hillary Rodham Clinton, 2009–present (Obama)

Treasury
None

Defense
None

Justice
Janet Reno, 1993–2001 (Clinton)

Interior
Gale Norton, 2001–2006 (Bush)

Agriculture
Ann Veneman, 2001–2005 (Bush)

Commerce
Juanita Kreps, 1977–1979 (Carter)
Barbara Franklin, 1992–1993 (Bush)

Labor
Frances Perkins, 1933–1945 (Roosevelt)
Ann McLaughlin, 1987–1989 (Reagan)
Elizabeth Dole, 1989–1991 (Bush)
Lynn Martin, 1991–1993 (Bush)
Alexis Herman, 1997–2001 (Clinton)
Elaine Chao, 2001–2009 (Bush)
Hilda Solis, 2009–present (Obama)

Health and Human Services (formerly Health, Education, and Welfare)
Oveta Culp Hobby, 1953–1955 (Eisenhower)
Patricia Roberts Harris, 1979–1981 (Carter)
Margaret Heckler, 1983–1985 (Reagan)
Donna Shalala, 1993–2001 (Clinton)
Kathleen Sebelius, 2009–present (Obama)

Housing and Urban Development
Carla Anderson Hills, 1975–1977 (Ford)
Patricia Roberts Harris, 1977–1979 (Carter)

Transportation
Elizabeth Dole, 1983–1987 (Reagan)
Mary Peters, 2006–2009 (Bush)

Energy
Hazel O'Leary, 1993–1997 (Clinton)

Education
Shirley Mount Hufstedler, 1979–1981 (Carter)
Margaret Spellings, 2005–2009 (Bush)

Veterans Affairs
None

Homeland Security
Janet Napolitano, 2009–present (Obama)

Women have made substantial gains in obtaining White House staff positions in recent years, particularly during the administrations of Bill Clinton, George W. Bush, and Barack Obama. However, a glass ceiling still seems to exist when it comes to the president's inner circle of advisers. Even when women are appointed to White House staff positions, their roles tend to be more political than related to the policymaking process in the White House.[45]

As national security adviser during Bush's first term and secretary of state during his second, Condoleezza Rice was a prominent exception to that rule. Rice played an integral role in drafting the Bush administration's foreign policy strategy in the war on terrorism as well as in planning the invasion of Iraq following the terrorist attacks on September 11, 2001. During the first Bush term, Rice was "by far the closest [adviser] to Bush" and thus of "critical importance" in helping Bush reach foreign policy decisions, particularly when other senior advisers were at odds over proposed courses of action: Rice "operated at the interface between the president and his political advisers on the one hand and his foreign policy team on the other."[46] However, notwithstanding the influence of Rice and Communications Director Karen Hughes, another of Bush's most powerful advisers in the early years of his administration, no woman has yet served as a chief of staff and only a handful of women have ever earned the title, as Hughes did, of special assistant to the president.

Dee Dee Myers, who served as Clinton's first press secretary (and the first woman to ever hold the job), was certainly a visible member of the Clinton team due to the daily press briefings she conducted. However, she had difficulty performing her duties as she was routinely excluded from the inner circle and access to certain information available to Clinton's closest advisers. Situational and structural barriers also exist for women seeking top staff positions in the White House. Not only do women with family responsibilities realize many political career opportunities somewhat later in life than their male counterparts, much of the White House staff comes from the president's campaign staff, where women rarely play a major role.[47] Hughes, who was a close adviser to Bush as communications director during his 2000 campaign as well as the first two years of his administration, left her position to return to her home state of Texas while her son was in high school. (She did, however, continue to play an advisory role from afar during the president's reelection campaign during 2004, and would go on to serve as undersecretary of state for public diplomacy from 2005 to 2007.)[48] Similarly, Valerie Jarrett served as a close aide to Obama during his presidential campaign before becoming a senior adviser in the White House.

The First Lady

The role of the first lady, as wife of the president, is a private one with public duties. There is no constitutional mandate or description for the job, yet many first ladies have served their husbands "as policy advisers and political assistants—some privately, some more publicly."[49] The public role for first ladies has mostly been a social one, yet several first ladies during the twentieth century provide distinct examples of the power and influence that can come with the position. Each woman has been allowed to determine her own role within her husband's administration. Some, like Mamie Eisenhower, Lady Bird Johnson, Barbara Bush, and Laura Bush, have opted for more traditional, nonpublic roles. Others, like Edith Wilson, Eleanor Roosevelt, Rosalyn Carter, and Hillary Rodham Clinton, opted for active involvement in policy decisions and publicly acknowledged their political roles within the administration. To date, Michelle Obama—a Princeton- and Harvard-educated attorney who stepped away from her career during her husband's presidential campaign—has taken a more traditional view of the first lady's role in supporting nonpolitical causes such as support for military families, yet she does advocate for certain issues on her husband's policy agenda.

Although each first lady shapes her own role within the White House, the fundamental duties of the modern first lady include some or all of the following: wife and mother, public figure and celebrity, the nation's social hostess, symbol of US womanhood, White House manager and preservationist, campaigner, champion of social causes, presidential spokesperson, presidential and political party booster, diplomat, and political and presidential partner.[50] The Office of the First Lady has become, in recent years, part of the official organizational structure of the Office of the President. One of the main responsibilities of the first lady's staff is to deal with the day-to-day needs of the news media. In addition to employing a press secretary, most first ladies also have a chief of staff, a social secretary, a projects director (for causes that a first lady may adopt, such as literacy in the case of Barbara Bush), and several other special assistants. Since the 1970s, first ladies have employed anywhere between twelve to twenty-eight full-time staff members.[51]

Perhaps no one has so stretched the boundaries of national expectation for the president's wife as Hillary Rodham Clinton, who made history in 2000 when she won a US Senate seat in New York. She writes in her memoirs that first ladies have a position but not a real job: "There is no training manual for First Ladies. . . . Like all First Ladies before me, I had to decide what I wanted to do with the opportunities and responsibilities I had inherited."[52] As a successful attorney with her own political ambitions and an active role in policy decisions, Clinton proved to be both an asset and a liability during her husband's presidential campaigns and two terms in office. From the early days of Clinton's first presidential campaign, when he told voters that they would get "two for the price of one" if he were elected, so-called Hillary bashing became routine in the media as many political pundits questioned whether she planned to act as a copresident.[53] The only first lady to choose an office among the president's top advisers in the West Wing of the White House, she signaled from the start her intention to be a full partner in the presidency with her husband.

Soon after her husband's inauguration, Clinton accepted a formal position within the White House as chair of the president's Task Force on National Health Reform. Two other first ladies had also held formal positions, including Eleanor Roosevelt as the assistant director for the Office of Civilian Defense from September 1941 to February 1942 and Rosalyn Carter as honorary chairman of the President's Commission on Mental Health from February 1977 to April 1978. But unlike theirs, Clinton's appointment to oversee the creation of the task force gave tremendous political influence and formal power over a major area of domestic policy to a first lady. Bill Clinton had made reforming the nation's health care system a major issue during his campaign, and he touted his wife's experience as chair of various policy-related committees during his tenure as governor of Arkansas as evidence that she was the best possible person for the job. In spite of her previous political experience, however, the challenge of reforming the nation's health care system proved to be too much for the first lady. Although she was given high praise for both the task force report and her testimony before Congress, health care reform was considered "dead on arrival" on Capitol Hill by the end of the congressional session in 1994. As a result, Clinton lowered her political public profile and embraced more traditional activities for a first lady like working on social programs. Not until 2000, when she ran for the US Senate, did Clinton "again lay claim to formal political power."[54]

■ **Governors and Other Statewide Positions**

State governors have served many important political functions throughout the history of the United States. Not only are they key players in the implementation of public policy at the state level, but they also serve as liaisons in the creation of federal policies that impact the state funding of programs. This role became crucial in the 1990s, as Congress gave more control and responsibility to states in the implementation of major federal programs like welfare. As a result, governors perhaps hold more power and influence now than ever before, not only in overseeing their state budgets and bureaucracies but in policymaking in Washington, D.C., as well. Like the presidency, governorships have also been traditionally male bastions of power; in fact, four of the last six men elected president were state governors (Carter, Reagan, Clinton, and Bush).

Women have historically not had an easy time winning their state's highest political office, and many women gubernatorial candidates have been harmed by negative attitudes and stereotypes suggesting that a woman could not succeed in such a powerful executive position. Since so few women have served as state governors, research to determine the leadership styles of women in this position or trends in their impact on policymaking has yet to provide definitive answers. However, the face of the state governor is finally starting to change.[55] Recent trends have shown that most women running for governor have previous political experience at either the local or state level and that they are most successful when running in open-seat elections (as opposed to races against incumbents).[56] According to another study that considers the impact of gender on gubernatorial personality and the exertion of political power, female governors are more likely than male governors to take a "feminine" approach to their public duties—empowering others to participate in the political process as opposed to wielding power—yet they are just as willing to take a more "masculine," top-down approach when necessary to adapt to the traditionally male-dominated political environment.[57]

As of 2009, a total of six women were serving as state governors. The figure peaked in 2004 and 2007, when nine women served in the position simultaneously. A total of thirty-one women have served as governor (nineteen Democrats and twelve Republicans) in twenty-three states. Of those, twenty were elected in their own right, three replaced their husbands, and eight became governor by constitutional succession. Arizona is the only state where a woman governor has ever been succeeded by another woman; it boasts the largest number—four—of women to hold the position. Rose Mofford, a Democrat, was elected secretary of state in 1986, and succeeded to governor in 1988 after the impeachment and conviction of Governor Evan Mecham. Mofford served as governor until 1991. Jane Dee Hull, a Republican, also began her ascent to governor as the Arizona secretary of state; she reached office in 1997 upon the resignation of Fife Symington, who had been convicted of fraud. Hull was elected to a full term in 1998, when Arizona became the only state to have an all-female line of succession, as women held the offices of governor, secretary of state (Betsey Bayless), attorney general (Janet Napolitano), treasurer (Carol Springer), and superintendent of public instruction (Lisa Graham Keegan). Janet Napolitano, a Democrat who made Senator John Kerry's short list for running mate in the 2004 presidential contest, succeeded Hull as governor in 2003. In 2009, when Napolitano became secretary of homeland security, she was succeeded by the lieutenant governor, Jan Brewer.[58]

Although the governorship of large states is one of the most likely stepping stones to the White House, only one of the six largest electoral states (California, New York, Texas, Florida, Illinois, and Pennsylvania) has ever elected a woman as governor: Democrat Ann Richards was elected as the governor of Texas in 1990 but defeated by George W. Bush in her reelection effort in 1994. (Richards is the second woman governor in Texas; Miriam Amanda "Ma" Ferguson, a Democrat, served as governor from

1925 to 1927 and 1933 to 1935, replacing her husband, who was impeached.) Nellie Tayloe Ross, a Wyoming Democrat, became the nation's first woman governor in 1925, replacing her husband after he died in office. Ross served for two years and then became vice chair of the Democratic National Committee and director of the US Mint. At the 1928 Democratic National Convention, she received thirty-one votes on the first ballot for vice president. Ella Grasso, a Democrat from Connecticut who served from 1975 to 1980, was the first woman elected as governor in her own right. Republicans would not elect their first woman governor until 1986, Kay A. Orr of Nebraska.

Other statewide positions serve as important political stepping stones for women who seek the office of governor or an even higher elected political office. At the time of this writing in 2009, eight women served as state lieutenant governor, thirteen as secretary of state, four as state attorney general, ten as state treasurer, eight as state auditor, and four as state controller. In addition, five states have women in the office of chief education official, and fourteen women serve in other statewide offices. Nationwide, women hold seventy-two of the 314 statewide elective positions, or 22.9 percent (fifty Democrats, twenty-one Republicans, and one independent). Historically, every state except Maine (which only elects the governor) has elected at least one woman to statewide office.[59]

■ Mayors

Historically, women have played a much larger role in local politics. Many women who have had successful political careers at a much higher level began their careers in elected positions at the city level. In 1887, Susanna Salter of Argonia, Kansas, was elected the nation's first woman mayor. Bertha K. Landes was a Republican city council president when she became acting mayor of Seattle in 1924, the first woman to lead a major US city. Two years later she was elected mayor in her own right in a campaign run by women, but lost in her bid for a second full term. As of 2009, a total of 193 women were serving as mayors of cities with populations of 30,000 or more. Of these, the woman who heads the largest city is Stephanie Rawlings-Baker of Baltimore, Maryland, which has a population of more than 650,000. Other women mayors of major cities include Mayor Ashley Swearengin of Fresno, California, Mayor Shirley Franklin of Atlanta, Georgia, and Mayor Kathryn L. Taylor of Tulsa, Oklahoma; see, for example, Table 6.2.

Dallas, Texas, is the largest city in the nation to ever elect a woman mayor (it currently ranks ninth among cities, with a population of more than 1.2 million), and it has done so three times. For instance, Laura Miller was elected mayor in 2002 after serving for three and a half years on the city council; she served as mayor until 2007, when she decided not to seek reelection. Miller's agenda while mayor was diverse; she showed support for business interests such as a revitalization project in downtown Dallas and a new convention center but also supported the social needs of citizens with initiatives for affordable housing and a new intake cen-

Table 6.2   Twenty Largest US Cities by Population with Women Mayors, 2010

Mayor	City	Population
Stephanie Rawlings-Blake	Baltimore, MD	651,154
Ashley Swearengin	Fresno, CA	427,652
Shirley Franklin	Atlanta, GA	416,474
Kathryn L. Taylor	Tulsa, OK	393,049
Pam Iorio	Tampa, FL	303,447
Ann Johnston	Stockton, CA	243,771
Yvonne J. Johnson	Greensboro, NC	223,891
Elaine M. Scruggs	Glendale, AZ	218,812
Cheryl Cox	Chula Vista, CA	203,000
Mary Verner	Spokane, WA	195,629
Debra McCartt	Amarillo, TX	173,627
Konstantina B. Lukes	Worcester, MA	172,648
Rhine L. McLin	Dayton, OH	166,179
Susan Gorin	Santa Rosa, CA	159,980
Molly Joseph Ward	Hampton, VA	146,437
Charmaine Tavares	Maui, HI	140,000
Kitty Piercy	Eugene, OR	137,893
Janet Taylor	Salem, OR	136,924
Lori Holt Pfeiler	Escondido, CA	133,559
Carolyn V. Cavecche	Orange, CA	128,821

Source: Center for American Women and Politics, Rutgers, The State University of New Jersey.

ter for the city's homeless population. Prior to entering Dallas city politics, Miller was a newspaper reporter for several papers, including the *Dallas Morning News*, the *New York Daily News*, and the *Miami Herald*, as well as alternative newspaper the *Dallas Observer*. While working as a journalist, she wrote columns in which she routinely took city officials to task for their incompetence and malfeasance. While mayor, she earned a reputation as a pragmatic if sometimes abrasive politician. Although not the first woman mayor of Dallas—where leadership had always come from the male-dominated worlds of oil, real estate, and other corporate sectors—Miller challenged the status quo with her independent style of leadership.[60] And by doing so, she strengthened the power of the mayor's office, which the Dallas elite had viewed as a merely ceremonial position.

Studies on the impact of women mayors suggest that there may be more gendered expectations for a woman to lead differently than there are measurable gendered differences. Given the nature of local politics and the types of social issues that mayors must deal with, policy issues at the city level might be more easily labeled "feminine" than "masculine." For example, education and social welfare programs are critical issues for cities and often benefit under leadership qualities associated with femininity and nurturing. This view of leadership at the city level calls into question the notion of "masculine" executive leadership.[61] However, as with research on women in higher executive political positions, research conducted as more women enter local office will provide a clearer picture of the impact that they may bring to the political process as executive leaders.

■ **Conclusion**

Although women have certainly made progress during the past decade in breaking down barriers to executive positions of political power, reaching gender parity is still many years away. However, the visibility of women in such integral national positions as secretary of state (Madeleine Albright, Condoleezza Rice, and Hillary Rodham Clinton), attorney general (Janet Reno), and national security adviser (Condoleezza Rice) can help change social and cultural attitudes toward women in positions of governmental power. The election of more women state governors is also crucial to increase the number of women on the short list of presidential and vice presidential candidates in future campaigns. Scholars have begun to focus more intently on the consequences of the domination of "masculine" executive politics. These include a loss of talent as the candidate pool is limited to men only, a constrained worldview with a limited set of experiences for solving problems, and a loss of governmental legitimacy in the eyes of women voters. An absence of women in executive political positions also perpetuates the myth that politics is a male-only arena.[62]

Despite all the progress made by women seeking political careers, the United States still lags behind several other countries, some with much more conservative political cultures, in terms of electing women to executive leadership positions. Although no other national system of government matches the constitutional uniqueness found within the US system of government, other countries have nonetheless selected women as their chief executives (including Great Britain, Ireland, Chile, Liberia, the Philippines, Israel, Argentina, Iceland, Pakistan, Nicaragua, and Sri Lanka). Many of these women were elected prime minister through a parliamentary system of government, which means that they did not have to win election through the support of a national constituency of voters. Instead, they only needed to win their local legislative seat and then gain the support of their party colleagues in parliament. However, societal expectations are beginning to change for women in US politics, and as more women enter executive political positions in the post-Clinton era, whether through election or appointment, the United States may continue to move even closer to its first woman president.

■ Study/Discussion Questions

1. How do executive political positions differ from legislative positions? Why is the executive branch known as a male-dominated institution?

2. What obstacles do women face in pursuing executive leadership positions, both in the corporate world and in national and state politics?

3. When will the United States elect its first woman presi-

dent? What changes might a woman bring to the executive branch and the White House?

4. How important are cabinet members and presidential advisers in the day-to-day operation of the White House? How have women made a difference in these positions in recent years?

5. How influential should a first lady be in her husband's administration? What will be the role of the eventual first husband?

6. Why have so few women ever served as state governors? What impact do women governors have on the political process?

7. How does the job of a mayor affect the notion of masculine executive leadership?

■ Online Resources

Advancing Women. http://www.advancingwomen.com.
The First Ladies Gallery. http://www.whitehouse.gov/history/ firstladies.
Institute for Women's Leadership. http://www.womensleadership .com.
The Institute for Women's Leadership at Rutgers University. http://iwl.rutgers.edu.
The White House Project. http://www.thewhitehouseproject.org.

■ Notes

1. Clinton became the first woman to win a presidential nominating contest when she won the New Hampshire primary in January 2008, which also earned her delegates to the national convention. Democrat Shirley Chisholm won a nonbinding, so-called beauty contest primary in New Jersey in 1972 that awarded no delegates.
2. Duerst-Lahti, "Reconceiving Theories of Power," 12.
3. Wilson, *Closing the Leadership Gap*, 8.
4. For example, see Helgesen, *The Female Advantage*, and Deemer and Fredericks, *Dancing on the Glass Ceiling*.
5. Helgesen, *The Female Advantage*, 3.
6. Book, *Why the Best Man for the Job Is a Woman*, 15–16.
7. Ibid., 2–5.
8. Ibid., 8–14.
9. Eagly and Johannesen-Schmidt, "The Leadership Styles of Women and Men," 795.

10. Those companies include Kraft Foods, Xerox, PepsiCo, TJX, Dupont, Yahoo, Avon Products, Sara Lee, Rite Aid, Archer Daniels Midland, Reynolds American, Western Union, Wellpoint, Sunoco, and BJ's Wholesale Club.

11. Sellers, "Most Powerful Women in Business."

12. Wilson, *Closing the Leadership Gap*, 53.

13. Tischler, "Where Are the Women?" 52.

14. Barnett, "Women, Leadership, and the Natural Order," 154–156.

15. Ibid., 156–158.

16. Duerst-Lahti, "Reconceiving Theories of Power," 18.

17. Conway et al., *Women and Political Participation*, 100.

18. DeConde, *Presidential Machismo*, 5.

19. Cronin and Genovese, *The Paradoxes of the American Presidency*, 105.

20. Greenstein, "George W. Bush and the Ghosts of Presidents Past," 77–80.

21. Han, "Presidential Leadership," 171.

22. Wayne, *The Road to the White House 2008*, 202.

23. Ibid., 203–204.

24. For a discussion on this trend in news coverage, see Patterson, *Out of Order*, and Sabato, *Feeding Frenzy*.

25. Cronin and Genovese, *The Paradoxes of the American Presidency*, 32–37.

26. Bystrom, "On the Way to the White House," 104.

27. Cronin and Genovese, *The Paradoxes of the American Presidency*, 31.

28. Waterman, Wright, and St. Clair, *The Image-Is-Everything Presidency*, 39–42.

29. Falk and Jamieson, "Changing the Climate of Expectations," 45–47.

30. See Fox and Lawless, "Entering the Arena?"

31. Polsby and Wildavsky, *Presidential Elections*, 143–145.

32. See Kenski and Falk, "Of What Is This Glass Ceiling Made?"

33. Wilson, *Closing the Leadership Gap*, 36.

34. Heith, "The Lipstick Watch," 123–124.

35. For example, see CBS News, "Ready for a Woman President?"; Powell, "Poll Finds Readiness for Female President," A1; and Smith, "Voters Think U.S. Ready for Woman as President," A5. In addition, a February 2005 poll by the Siena College Research Institute found that six out of ten voters were ready for a woman president and that 81 percent of those surveyed would vote for a woman president. Potential candidates for 2008 who topped the survey included Clinton, Rice, and Senator Elizabeth Dole (R-NC).

36. Green, "The Front-Runner's Fall."

37. Clift and Brazaitis, *Madam President*, 28.

38. Marks, "The Quest of Carol Moseley Braun," 1.

39. Democrat Shirley Chisholm won a nonbinding, so-called beauty contest primary in New Jersey in 1972 that awarded no delegates.

40. Michigan and Florida were so-called beauty contests with no delegates awarded, while Texas held both a primary (which Clinton won) and a caucus (which Obama won). In addition, although Clinton's victory by popular vote in New Hampshire was seen as a major comeback after she lost the Iowa caucus, she and Obama earned an equal number of delegates in the state. Similarly, although Clinton won the popular vote in Nevada, Obama actually won more delegates (by one).

41. An estimate by RealClearPolitics.com, since Iowa, Nevada, Maine, and Washington did not release official vote totals; http://www.realclearpolitics.com/epolls/2008/president/democratic_vote_count.html.

42. Martin, *The Presidency and Women*, 6–7.

43. Borrelli, *The President's Cabinet*, 214.

44. Tenpas, "Women on the White House Staff," 91.

45. Ibid., 92–93.

46. Mann, *Rise of the Vulcans*, 315.

47. Ibid., 99–101.

48. O'Connor, "Hughes Answers the Call," E1.

49. Burrell, "The Office of the First Lady and Public Policymaking," 169.

50. Watson, *The Presidents' Wives*, 72.

51. Ibid., 112–113.

52. Clinton, *Living History*, 119.

53. Winfield, "The First Lady, Political Power, and the Media," 166–179.

54. See Borrelli, "The First Lady as Formal Advisor to the President."

55. Marshall and Mayhead, "The Changing Face of the Governorship," 14.

56. See Wier, "Women Governors in the 21st Century," 226–237.

57. See Barth and Ferguson, "Gender and Gubernatorial Personality."

58. Center for American Women and Politics, "Statewide Elective Executive Women 2009."

59. Ibid.

60. Nichols, "From Muckraker to Mayor."

61. Tolleson-Rinehart, "Do Women Leaders Make a Difference?" 149–165.

62. Duerst-Lahti, "Reconceiving Theories of Power," 25.

7

Women in the Judiciary

I have been called the most powerful woman in the United States.
■ Sandra Day O'Connor,
former associate justice of the US Supreme Court

Who is the most powerful woman in the United States? Several women in both the political and corporate worlds would probably top the list, but US Supreme Court Associate Justice Sandra Day O'Connor was certainly among them while she was on the bench. She herself has stated that many people believe that as the first woman appointed to the nation's highest court, she wielded tremendous power over the governing process. During the 1980 presidential campaign, Ronald Reagan promised that if he were elected, he would nominate the first woman to the US Supreme Court. During his first year in office, he made good on that promise by nominating O'Connor, who was then a member of the Arizona State Court of Appeals. Despite having graduated third in her class from Stanford Law School, one of the top law schools in the nation, in 1952 (former Chief Justice William Rehnquist graduated first in the same class), O'Connor had experienced a difficult time finding work as an attorney in private practice. Instead, she embarked on a career of mostly public positions, including assistant state attorney general and Arizona state senator.

Upon O'Connor's historic appointment to the Supreme Court, Reagan was criticized by both liberals and conservatives for his choice. Liberals were happy to see the first woman join

143

the high court, but feared that her positions, particularly on women's issues, would be too conservative. Conservatives, by contrast, feared that she lacked adequate federal judicial experience and knowledge of the US Constitution and that she would uphold abortion rights (Reagan had also campaigned to make abortion illegal). When she retired from the Court nearly twenty-five years later, O'Connor had earned a reputation as a pragmatic and often centrist judge who held the swing vote on issues like abortion, affirmative action, and privacy rights.[1] She remained the only woman to serve on the high court until Ruth Bader Ginsburg, appointed by President Bill Clinton, joined her in 1993. Ginsburg, often outspoken on the issue of equal rights for women, complained in 2007 of being lonely on the Court following O'Connor's retirement.[2] In 2009, she would be joined by the third woman and the first Latina to sit on the nation's highest court after Barack Obama successfully nominated Sonia Sotomayor.

Women's ability to lead within the judicial branch of government is somewhat different than it is in other political arenas. While many judges at the state level are elected, the president nominates all judges at the federal level. Judges must follow a formal process for interpreting and applying the law (as opposed to legislators who create laws), which sometimes limits their ability to directly shape public policy. Good judges are also supposed to be impartial and independent when deciding cases, putting party and ideology aside. Whether they are always able to do so is difficult to determine; however, one might assume that a feminist judge would have a harder time changing the legal culture of the United States if she were to stay true to her impartial judicial traditions. In terms of recruitment, judges do not have as high a profile as other politicians, which means that female role models within the judiciary are harder to find. This chapter considers the progress women have made in the legal profession, the history of women's judgeships at both the federal and state level, and the impact that women make on the judiciary as a whole. What is the historical relationship between women and the law in the United States? What barriers, if any, still exist for women entering the legal profession or seeking judicial posts? And, most importantly, do women judges make a difference in their interpretation and application of the law?

▪ Women and the Law

The rule of law, or adherence to the basic legal structure of a society, is fundamental to the US constitutional system of government. Yet for most of the nation's history, women did not have access to the law and the tools that it provided in shaping the political system. As we discussed in Chapter 2, not only did women not have a part in drafting the US Constitution, they received no specific mention anywhere in the document. In addition, since the founding era, the "legal status of women has been shaped by an ideology grounded in cultural and physical differences between the sexes."[3]

The legal disenfranchisement of women in US life lasted well into the twentieth century, despite the ratification in 1868 of the Fourteenth Amendment, which declares equal protection under and due process of the laws. In 1875, the US Supreme Court "dismissed out-of-hand" the claim that women had a constitutional right to vote as equal citizens. Also in the late nineteenth century, it upheld state laws barring women from practicing law and even from working as bartenders unless they were members of the owner's immediate family. These rulings only reinforced the image of women as second-class citizens. In the early twentieth century, the Court also handed down rulings, now seen as paternalistic, to protect women in the workplace with regard to hours, working conditions, and wages. At the time, it was commonly assumed that women were not the equals of men in the workplace; therefore, the supposed problem of women working outside the home needed to be dealt with. The Court would not begin to reverse its views on gender-based discrimination in the workplace until the early 1970s.[4]

Women were also the victims of discrimination in various other legal forms until the latter part of the twentieth century. Based on common law traditions brought with the original colonists from England, women lost all legal and property rights upon marriage. Married women were denied equal custody rights, the right to keep their wages, and the right to divorce; single women also had few legal rights. Up until the early twentieth century, when many of these state laws began to be rescinded, married women were considered the legal property of their husbands, a view reinforced by a 1905 ruling by the US Supreme Court that

stated a husband could sue for property damages if his wife committed adultery. By losing their legal identity upon marriage,
women were also banned from entering into legal contracts
(which meant they could not pursue opportunities as business
owners), and they could not file a suit in a court of law.

Women were also excluded as jurors for decades after they
received the right to vote in 1920, even though jury duty is considered one of the most important civic responsibilities of US citizens. Even into the 1960s and 1970s, several states granted automatic exemptions to women for jury service, which meant that
they still had laws excluding women as jurors. The issue was finally settled in 1975 when the Supreme Court ruled in *Taylor v.
Louisiana* that the exclusion of women violated the Sixth
Amendment to the US Constitution, which mandated a jury of
one's peers; if women were eliminated, a cross section of the population could not be adequately represented.

Only since the 1960s have women gained access to the law as
equal citizens, as professionials, and as agents of political change.
Spurred on by the modern women's movement, laws (whether
through congressional action or rulings by the US Supreme
Court) finally began to equate women's legal status with that of
men in the areas of property and economic rights, employment
rights, and educational rights. As radical feminist and legal scholar
Catharine A. MacKinnon notes:

> Law in the United States is at once a powerful medium and a
> medium for power. Backed by force, it is also an avenue for
> demand, a vector of access, an arena for contention other than the
> physical, a forum for voice, a mechanism for accountability, a form
> for authority, and an expression of norms. Women seeking change
> for women have found that all these consequences and possibilities
> cannot be left to those elite men who have traditionally dominated
> in and through law, shaping its structures and animating attitudes
> to guarantee the supremacy of men as a group over women in
> social life. Women who work with law have learned that, while a
> legal change may not always make a social change, sometimes it
> helps, and law unchanged can make social change impossible.[5]

■ Women and the Legal Profession

Although many paths can lead a person into a political career, a
legal career—either as an attorney or judge—is a common path to

elected or appointed office at the state or national level. Women were mostly excluded from the legal profession itself until the early 1970s. Title IX of the Education Act of 1972, which guaranteed equal access to academic and athletic resources regardless of gender, dramatically increased the number of women attending law school. By 2008, women represented nearly half (47.3 percent) of all first-year law students in the United States and 31.6 percent (more than 360,000) of all attorneys.[6]

Studies and surveys within the legal profession have shown that women attorneys face many obstacles to achieving top leadership positions in law firms, corporations, and governmental agencies. Although overt sex discrimination may not be the biggest problem that women attorneys face in career advancement, there are organizational, institutional, and systemic obstacles, including gender-based assumptions and practices, a lack of mentoring, and family-work conflicts.[7] In a study by the American Bar Association's Commission on Women in the Profession, women's opportunities within the legal profession, like those within the political and corporate worlds, are limited by unconscious stereotypes, inadequate access to support networks, inflexible workplace structures, sexual harassment, and bias in the justice system.[8] For example, in 2008, women held only 18.4 percent of general counsel positions in Fortune 500 companies.[9]

Gender stereotypes are particularly problematic for women attorneys, who "often do not receive the same presumption of competence or commitment as their male colleagues."[10] A majority of women in the profession believe they are held to higher standards than men (a problem compounded for minority women). The lack of balance between work and family life also hampers career paths for women, including a double standard for working mothers who are criticized for their lack of professional commitment if they do not sacrifice family for work. Although no evidence exists to suggest that women attorneys with family responsibilities are any less committed to their careers, they are more likely to leave large law firms for jobs that offer more flexible work schedules.[11]

Systemic gender bias within the justice system has long remained a problem for women, litigants as well as attorneys. Beginning in the 1980s, several initiatives were put forth to address some of these problems. Courts as institutions are quite traditional and formal in practice, and changes often occur slowly.

For example, some courts used to sanction married women attorneys who refused to use their husband's last name. While most cases of blatant discrimination are now rare, subtle discrimination still occurs in regard to the demographics of the bench, bar, and court personnel; gender differences in rulings on bail hearings and custody awards; and the general perception of participants based on gender (and also race).[12]

Most often, bias in the justice system falls into one of three categories: disrespectful treatment (for example, addressing female but not male attorneys by their first names, mistaking female attorneys for support staff, or ignoring them as insignificant to the proceedings); dismissive attitudes that discredit cases involving women, thereby adding insult to injury (be they matters of sexual harassment, employment discrimination, or acquaintance rape, for example); and stereotyping based on gender, race, ethnicity, disability, and/or sexual orientation (examples include the assumptions that domestic violence victims are somehow responsible for provoking their abuse and that mothers who work full-time are less deserving of child custody). As a result, many states have implemented codes of conduct and educational programs to eliminate gender and racial bias in the courtroom.[13]

■ Women as Federal Judges

Today, more than a hundred courts make up the federal judicial branch. The lowest federal courts are the district courts, which serve as trial courts with juries; these are where most federal cases originate. If a district court case is appealed, it moves up to a federal court of appeals. There are twelve federal judicial circuits (or territories), and each has its own court of appeals. With the exception of the District of Columbia, which has its own circuit, each includes at least three states. Nine justices sit on the US Supreme Court (composed of eight associate justices and the chief justice), and, like other federal judges, all are appointed to life terms. Justices and federal judges can be impeached by a majority vote in the House of Representatives and removed by a two-thirds majority vote in the Senate. This has never happened to a Supreme Court justice; all have served until retirement or death. When a vacancy occurs on any federal court, a potential replacement is nominated by the president. The Senate Judiciary Committee considers the nomination; if approved, it goes to the entire Senate, which confirms it by a simple majority vote. Since justices and federal judges serve life terms, the nomination process constitutes an important opportunity for presidents to enjoy a lasting political legacy.

However, the "integration of women into the federal judiciary has been achingly slow."[14] President Franklin D. Roosevelt appointed the first woman to a federal bench: Florence Ellinwood Allen, appointed in 1934, served on the Sixth Circuit Court of Appeals for twenty-five years. No other woman would be appointed to a court of appeals for thirty-four years until 1968, when Lyndon Johnson nominated Shirley Ann Mount Hufstedler to the Ninth Circuit Court of Appeals (where she served until 1979). Burnita Shelton Matthews became the first woman to serve on a US district court when Harry Truman issued her a recess appointment in the District of Columbia in October 1949. The Senate confirmed her nomination in April 1950. John F. Kennedy appointed one woman to a district court position, and Johnson appointed two women to district courts. Richard Nixon and Gerald Ford appointed one woman each to a federal judgeship, both to district courts, making no appointments to an appeals court.

Jimmy Carter was the first president to seriously increase the number of women serving in the judiciary, having "both the interest and the opportunity to diversify the federal courts" in terms of gender, race, and ethnicity.[15] He appointed a total of forty women to the federal judiciary (twenty-nine to district courts, which equaled 14.3 percent of his appointments, and eleven, or 19.6 percent, to courts of appeal). Carter did not have the opportunity to appoint a justice to the Supreme Court during his four years in the White House, even though presidents have historically had opportunities to make appointments every two years on average. Carter's immediate successors, Ronald Reagan and George H. W. Bush, appointed fewer women to the federal bench. Reagan, who disapproved of using affirmative action policies in judicial appointments, named a total of thirty women to federal judgeships (twenty-four, or 8.3 percent, to district courts and six, or 7.2 percent, to courts of appeal). Bush appointed a total of thirty-six women to the federal bench (twenty-nine, or 19.6 percent, to district courts and seven, or 16.7 percent, to courts of appeal).

Bill Clinton, however, reversed that trend by appointing 108 women to federal judicial posts (eighty-eight, or 28.9 percent, to district courts and twenty, or 30.3 percent, to courts of appeal). During his eight years in office, George W. Bush appointed a total of seventy-one women to the federal bench (fifty-four, or 20.7 percent, to district courts and seventeen, or 27.9 percent, to courts of appeal). (See Table 7.1.) He also became the first president to nominate to the Supreme Court a woman who would not be confirmed (as we will discuss). As of March 2010, Barack Obama had appointed two women to courts of appeal, and six women to district courts.

Historically, few women have been appointed to federal judicial positions. The main reason is that up until the 1970s, few women had entered the legal profession. So, as was the case for leadership positions in the legislative and executive branches, a limited pool of qualified women candidates existed. Bias has also existed in the selection and confirmation process. Applicants whose careers have focused on public service or public interest law are assumed to be activists on certain policy issues, thus inclined as judges to go beyond merely interpreting the law to actively participate in making new law. Judicial activists can adhere to either a liberal or conservative political ideology. For example, liberal activists view the Constitution as a broad grant of freedom to citizens against government interference, particularly with respect to civil rights and civil liberties. Judicial activism is not viewed favorably by those who believe that judges should leave policymaking to elected officials. Women, particularly women of color, disproportionately come from public service backgrounds and are thus often overlooked for appointments.[16]

Two other important factors have contributed to the small number of women in judicial positions. First, the qualifications in terms of education and experience are high. Most candidates must not only hold a law degree but have several years of trial experience as well. Second, the judicial selection process is complicated and is often tied to strong professional relationships and reputations within male-dominated legal circles. As a result, many women do not find themselves on the short lists for consideration.[17] Two recent nominations to the Supreme Court—Harriet Miers by George W. Bush and Sonia Sotomayor by Barack Obama—provide interesting and somewhat contradictory

Table 7.1 Presidential Appointments of Women to the Federal Judiciary, 1933–2010

President	District Court		Appeals Court		Supreme Court	
	No. of Women/Total	Percentage	No. of Women/Total	Percentage	No. of Women/Total	Percentage
Franklin D. Roosevelt	0/134	0	1/51	2.0	0/8	0
Harry S. Truman	1/101	1.0	0/27	0	0/4	0
Dwight D. Eisenhower	0/129	0	0/45	0	0/5	0
John F. Kennedy	1/102	1.0	0/21	0	0/2	0
Lyndon B. Johnson	2/126	1.6	1/40	2.5	0/2	0
Richard Nixon	1/181	0.6	0/46	0	0/4	0
Gerald Ford	1/50	2.0	0/11	0	0/1	0
Jimmy Carter	29/203	14.3	11/56	19.6	n/a	
Ronald Reagan	24/290	8.3	6/83	7.2	1/3	33.3
George H.W. Bush	29/148	19.6	7/42	16.7	0/2	0
Bill Clinton	88/305	28.9	20/66	30.3	1/2	50
George W. Bush	54/261	20.7	17/61	27.9	0/2	0
Barack Obama	6/10	60.0	2/6	33.3	1/1	100
Total	236/2040	11.6	65/555	11.7	3/36	8.3

Source: Federal Judges Biographical Database.

examples of how many of these factors play out in the confirmation process.

First, let's consider the many issues at play when the president
is faced with a vacancy on the high court. Presidents rely on many
factors in their decision to nominate someone, including objective
qualifications, policy preferences, political support, and personal
reward. The president's "situation" also affects the confirmation
process, including his political strength in the Senate and level of
public approval, the mobilization of interest groups, and the
importance of the nomination (for example, will a new justice
change the ideological balance of the Court?).[18] Nominees have
always been attorneys, although this is not a constitutional or
statutory requirement, and most have attended top law schools; of
the justices at the time of this writing, Antonin Scalia, Anthony
Kennedy, Stephen Breyer, and John Roberts attended Harvard;
Clarence Thomas, Samuel Alito, and Sonia Sotomayor attended
Yale; Ruth Bader Ginsburg graduated from Columbia after spending her first two years at Harvard; and John Paul Stevens attended
Northwestern. Previous jobs usually include appellate judgeships
(state or federal), jobs in the executive branch, jobs in the Justice
Department, or high elected offices. Each of the current justices
was nominated while serving on a US Court of Appeals. Most justices are older than fifty when nominated, and a majority are from
upper- or middle-upper-class families (Thomas and Sotomayor
are exceptions to the latter, having grown up in poorer, working-
class environments).[19]

Despite attempts to keep the Court an unbiased and independent institution, presidential appointments are political, and a
myth of merit exists when a president makes his selection. As a
result, several highly qualified individuals have been passed over
for appointment. Race, gender, religion, and geography all factor
into the nomination process. Several other considerations related
to the political climate can influence the president's decision as
well, like whether or not the president is from the same party as
the Senate majority and whether or not the president and his
nominee might face a tough confirmation battle.[20] Although the
nomination process has been democratized since 1968, it has also
become "disorderly, contentious, and unpredictable," a trend that
can be attributed to changes in political institutions in the past
thirty years that allow for greater public participation in the selec-

tion process.[21] What used to happen mostly behind the closed doors of the Senate is now a more political, campaign-like media event, with both opponents and supporters (most notably well-funded interest groups) arguing about whether or not a nominee's ideological perspective should disqualify him or her from service. In this environment, unanimous or near-unanimous confirmation votes in the Senate have become the exception rather than the rule, with senators in the minority party often voting against the nominee just to score political points with their constituents or supporters instead of judging the nominee based on qualifications.

In the fall of 2005, George W. Bush nominated White House Counsel Harriet Miers to the Supreme Court to fill the vacancy created by Sandra Day O'Connor's retirement. Initially, John Roberts had been nominated to fill O'Connor's seat, but he was instead nominated for chief justice following the death of William Rehnquist in September 2005. Miers was a surprise pick for several reasons, most notable among them the fact that she had never served as a judge, lacked experience with constitutional issues, and had close personal ties to Bush (an expectation exists that justices are to remain independent with no close ties to the president). While both liberals and conservatives voiced opposition over Miers's nomination, socially conservative and/or evangelical groups were most vocal; they had played a significant role in Bush's reelection in 2004, and in return, they wanted conservative, strict-constructionist judges who would not engage in what they believed amounted to judicial activism. Whereas Roberts had a long and impressive judicial track record with enough service on both federal district and appellate courts to please these conservative groups, Miers had no such track record and no judicial experience. After she fared poorly in interviews with senators and on the questionnaire provided by the Senate Judiciary Committee regarding her knowledge of the US Constitution, Miers withdrew her nomination in October 2005, only three weeks after Bush had nominated her and prior to any Senate confirmation hearings.[22] Appeals court judge Samuel Alito was then nominated and confirmed to fill O'Connor's vacancy.

As a result, Ginsburg was the only woman on the Supreme Court for nearly four years, until the confirmation of Sonia Sotomayor in August 2009. Due to the surprise retirement of Justice David Souter in May 2009, Barack Obama had the opportunity for a Supreme Court nomination within the first few months of his presidency. Many pundits predicted that he would nominate a woman, while others predicted that he would make history by nominating the first Hispanic to the high court. Obama opted for both with Sotomayor, whose impressive resume includes experience on the US District Court for the Southern District of New York (to which she was nominated by George H.W. Bush in 1991) and the Second Circuit Court of Appeals (nominated by Bill Clinton in 1997). Sotomayor, who is of Puerto Rican descent, earned her bachelor's degree with honors from Princeton University and her law degree from Yale Law School, where she also served as an editor of the *Yale Law Review*. Prior to her appointment to the district court, Sotomayor served as an assistant district attorney in New York and worked for several years in private practice. She has also been an adjunct law professor at both New York University and Columbia University.

In effect, Sotomayor was an outstanding nominee in terms of education and experience. But her nomination did receive opposition from many conservative Republicans in the Senate, who charged her with judicial activism despite the fact that her record on the federal bench suggested she was more moderate than liberal and who criticized her now-famous "wise Latina" remark. In 2001, while giving a talk at Berkeley Law School, Sotomayor remarked: "I would hope that a wise Latina woman with the richness of her experiences would more often than not reach a better conclusion than a white male who hasn't lived that life." The remark was taken somewhat out of context by Sotomayor's critics, who questioned her about it during her confirmation hearings before the Senate Judiciary Committee. She stated that although personal experiences help to shape a judge's perspective, ultimately the law is the only guide for making a decision. Sotomayor was confirmed by the Senate on August 6, 2009, by a vote of 68–31 (all opposition votes came from Republicans). The final vote in the Senate to confirm Sotomayor represents how the confirmation process has become more politicized and ideologically contentious since O'Connor's confirmation with a unanimous vote of 99–0 in 1981 and Ginsburg's in 1993 with a vote of 96–3. Many observers of the Supreme Court suggest that it would be hard to imagine the high court returning to an all-male lineup.

Ruth Bader Ginsburg: And Then There Were Two

Although her appointment was not as high profile as Sandra Day O'Connor's in 1981, Ruth Bader Ginsburg was nonetheless the first woman appointed to the Supreme Court by a Democrat, President Bill Clinton. Her 1993 appointment also meant that, for the first time, there was more than just one "women's seat" on the bench (although she was the only woman on the Court from 2006, when O'Connor retired, until 2009, when Sonia Sotomayor was confirmed). Ginsburg received her law degree from Columbia University in 1959 after completing her first two years of study at Harvard University. Like O'Connor, in spite of graduating at the top of her prestigious law school class (she tied for the number one spot), Ginsburg got her first job as a legal secretary. She then received a clerkship with a district court judge and worked for many years as a law school professor at both Rutgers University and Columbia University. She also worked as the general counsel for the American Civil Liberties Union from 1973 until 1980, when Jimmy Carter appointed her to the US Court of Appeals for the District of Columbia Circuit. She served as an appellate judge for thirteen years prior to her appointment to the Supreme Court.

When Clinton had his first opportunity to appoint a Supreme Court justice in 1993, Ginsburg's name appeared on the initial list of more than forty candidates being considered by the White House. Ginsburg's chances for appointment were improved by a campaign waged by her husband. Unknown to Ginsburg at the time, her husband Martin worked extensively behind the scenes to garner support for her in legal academic circles and major women's advocacy groups. His public relations strategy helped to secure his wife's position on the short list of candidates receiving serious consideration.[23] Ginsburg also made a lasting impression on Clinton when they met prior to her nomination. Clinton was impressed by Ginsburg's family struggles (her mother died of cancer when she was seventeen and her husband had also endured a battle with cancer early in their marriage) as well as her commitment to women's issues, in particular her fight against gender discrimination. Clinton stated that she was the perfect candidate for the high court due to her distinguished judicial career, her advocacy on behalf of women's issues, and her "demonstrated ability as a consensus builder [and] healer."[24]

Compared to the contentious and divisive confirmation of

continues

156

Ruth Bader Ginsburg *continued*

Clarence Thomas in 1991 (as discussed in Chapter 5), Ginsburg's was relatively smooth, with a 96–3 vote in the Senate. The Senate Judiciary Committee also welcomed two new members in 1993—just-elected Senators Dianne Feinstein (D-CA) and Carol Moseley Braun (D-IL). Ironically, despite Ginsburg's long support of women's issues and her prochoice stance, several women's groups were critical of her due to her belief, published in a law journal article, that the Court used the wrong rationale in its 1973 *Roe v. Wade* decision that legalized abortion. Ginsburg supported the outcome of the case but argued that a stronger constitutional argument could have been made. Some prochoice groups thus worried that she might support overturning the decision (an outcome that has not occurred).

According to legal scholar Lawrence Baum, Ginsburg has had little impact on the overall ideological balance of the conservative-leaning Courts of Rehnquist (1986–2005) and Roberts (2005–present). Ginsburg, a moderate liberal, is ideologically similar to the justice she replaced—Associate Justice Byron White, appointed by John F. Kennedy in 1962. Since she and fellow moderate liberal Stephen Breyer joined the court, "the proportion of pro–civil liberties decisions has increased only slightly . . . and the Court's doctrinal positions continue to be conservative in most respects."[25] Nonetheless, Ginsburg has strongly supported pro–affirmative action cases before the Court and has also continued her fight against gender discrimination in other ways as well. One of her most notable majority opinions came in 1996 with *United States v. Virginia*, in which the Court stated that the state-funded Virginia Military Institute's exclusion of women was unconstitutional, violating the equal protection clause of the Fourteenth Amendment.

Ginsburg, now in her second decade of service on the Court, has been an excellent role model for women who aspire to high-ranking judicial positions. Legal scholar Henry Abraham gives Ginsburg high praise for her time on the Court: "Always well prepared, an articulate, incisive questioner in oral argument, a clear and often elegant writer, Ruth Bader Ginsburg has proved herself to be a genuine asset on the Court."[26] As she herself stated at her inauguration to the Court on August 10, 1993: "A system of justice will be richer for diversity of background and experience. It will be poorer, in terms of appreciating what is at stake and the impact of its judgments, if all of its members are cast from the same mold."

■ Women, Courts, and the Policy Agenda

Women judges in the federal branch are important political actors for women's rights. As in other areas of politics, a woman engaged in judicial policymaking has the potential to bring a different perspective to the law. However, studies have not shown significant differences between the actions of female and male judges. According to legal scholar Anita Hill, "Empirical and anecdotal accounts do not conclusively establish the idea that individual women judge differently or that women as a group judge differently from men."[27] Still, a diverse judiciary in terms of sex, race, and ethnicity is important for symbolic reasons. Possible explanations for the results are that so few women have served as judges and that gender differences may be neutralized by the act of judging, which is bound to legal traditions and processes.[28] Diversity on the bench is also important "because the federal judiciary has been arguably the most important actor in women's rights." Both reproductive rights and gender equality are "judicially created rights," since they are not specifically guaranteed in the US Constitution but have been interpreted by the Supreme Court to exist.[29] A ruling by the Supreme Court can only be overturned by a constitutional amendment or if the Court overturns itself with a new decision.

The legal system places many institutional constraints on the members of the Supreme Court in their exercise of power. These include precedent, the parameters of constitutional and statutory law, concern for the integrity of the Court as an institution, and the decisionmaking process of the nine individuals who sit on the Court. Yet as Justice O'Connor points out, women on the bench can bring an important diversity to the selection of cases as well as the outcomes that affect policy: "None of this is to say that women do *not* differ from men in the way they exercise power, only that the differences are subtle. We all bring to the seats of power our individual experiences and values, and part of these depend on our gender."[30]

As discussed in Chapter 2, women have been viewed as occupants of the private (versus public) sphere since the nation's founding. Legally, women were denied property and identity separate from that of fathers or husbands, as well as other rights as equal citizens, into the twentieth century. The judicial system, and particularly the Supreme Court, relied for nearly two hundred years on biological essentialism to rule that women belonged only in the private sphere before changing course in the 1970s, when several decisions dealing with women's economic rights, workplace rights, and most notably reproductive rights showed that the Court was finally beginning to view women as legally equal to men.[31] In several cases throughout the 1970s and 1980s, it developed what is known as the intermediate or heightened scrutiny test to deal with sex-based discrimination. This meant that any law passed that places women in a separate category from men must be substantially related to an important government objective. As a result, the courts, and in particular the Supreme Court, have since been more sensitive to problems that women face in the workplace and in dealing with financial matters and have struck down certain discriminatory standards for women as unconstitutional.

■ Women as State and Local Judges

As part of the federal system of government, each state has its own system of courts. Although the exact structure may vary from state to state, states' judicial branches are generally similar to the federal branch, with lower trial courts, intermediate appellate courts, and a court of last appeal at the highest level (called supreme courts in most states). Only cases that deal with federal issues can be appealed from a state supreme court to the US Supreme Court. Although many people believe that the federal judiciary is the most important court system in the country, nearly 95 percent of all cases are heard in state courts. The selection of judges varies among states, with methods ranging from partisan elections (as in Texas), nonpartisan elections (as in Oregon and Washington), and political appointment with judicial retention (as in California, where a simple yes or no vote is cast to keep a governor's choice on the bench).

In 2009, 4,325 women were serving as state judges (26 percent of the 16,950 positions). Of those, 104 women judges (29 percent) were serving on state courts of last resort (usually the state's supreme court), 279 women judges (30 percent) sat on intermediate appellate courts, 2,440 women judges (23 percent) served on general jurisdiction courts, and 1,502 women judges (29 percent) were on limited and special jurisdiction courts.[32] In 1976, a total of twenty states had no women judges. During the Carter administration, when the president was actively appointing women and minorities to federal judicial positions, states began a similar trend. By 1979, each of the fifty states had at least one woman serving as a judge. Between 1980 and 1991, the percentage of women state judges increased from 4 to 9 percent. By 1991, among the 14,094 judges on state courts were 1,230 women.[33]

The increase in the number of women judges at the state level indicates a change in attitudes among voters in the states that elect and/or retain judges through the ballot box. It also suggests that the pool of eligible candidates for state judicial positions has grown in many states to include women attorneys, whose career paths can differ from that of their male colleagues (including, for example, more public sector work or work as a government lawyer). The demographics of the group of women now serving on state courts of last resort suggest that women are more often selected from lower state courts and have more experience as prosecutors than do their male counterparts. This trend suggests that "extensive judicial experience [may persuade] judicial selectors that nontraditional candidates are capable, despite the dissimilarity in their legal careers to [those of] more traditional white, male candidates."[34]

■ Do Women Judges Act Differently?

Although much more research is needed to make a strong and definitive argument, several studies since the 1980s point to ways in which women judges not only act differently than their male colleagues but otherwise make a difference in the outcome of specific cases or in the shaping of public policy. Compared to an earlier study showing that women trial judges generally did not convict or sentence felony defendants differently than men judges, a study of 30,000 felony cases from 1971 to 1979 showed that men judges took a more paternalistic view toward women defendants, whereas women judges were twice as likely to sentence female defendants to prison than their male colleagues.[35]

Other studies since have shown that women judges, regardless

160

Women on the California High Court:
Ideological Diversity in Action

California is the largest and most diverse state in the nation and is often noted for its progressive brand of politics, so the fact that it has yet to elect its first woman governor is surprising. However, the state's highest court cannot be criticized for being a male-dominated bench. Currently, three of the seven justices on the California Supreme Court are women. They include Associate Justice Joyce L. Kennard (appointed in 1989), Associate Justice Kathryn Mickle Werdegar (appointed in 1994), and Associate Justice Carol A. Corrigan (appointed in 2005). Corrigan, nominated by Governor Arnold Schwarzenegger, replaced Janice Rogers Brown, who now serves on the US Court of Appeals for the District of Columbia Circuit. In her time on the California Supreme Court, Brown was the only African American justice; notably more conservative than her six moderate Republican colleagues, she clashed often with Chief Justice Ronald M. George. As a result, she gained the attention of the Bush White House for a possible federal court position. Bush first nominated Brown to the appeals court in 2003, but Senate Democrats successfully blocked her nomination (along with a handful of other conservative Bush appointees to the federal bench) until 2005.

The most notable woman jurist in California's history, however, would have to be former Supreme Court chief justice Rose Elizabeth Bird. As the first woman ever to be appointed to California's highest court, in 1977, she served on the bench until January 1987. From the start, Bird had a distinguished career in both the law and public service. She received her law degree from Boalt Hall School of Law at the University of California–Berkeley in 1965, when only a handful of women were accepted to top law schools. She clerked for the chief justice of the Nevada Supreme Court after graduation, and, in 1966, she became the first woman hired as a deputy public defender in Santa Clara County. She taught at Stanford Law School from 1972 to 1974; in 1975, Governor Jerry Brown appointed her to be the first woman cabinet member in California. As secretary of the Agriculture and Services Agency, she had administrative responsibility over twelve different state agencies.

Under Bird's leadership, the Supreme Court strengthened

continues

Women on the California High Court *continued*

environmental laws, consumer rights, and the rights of women and minorities. Her accomplishments also included the 1984 adoption of the first rule to permit television and photographic coverage of court proceedings in trial and appellate courts with the consent of the presiding judge. Bird also introduced the first use of word and data processing into the courts. In 1986, she appointed the Committee on Gender Bias in the Courts, which began the trend for studies on treatment by state courts of people based on gender, race and ethnicity, sexual preferences, and disabilities.[36]

More important, Bird received national attention for her opposition to the death penalty, becoming a lightning rod on the issue by invalidating every one of the fifty-eight death penalty cases that she heard on appeal. Supporters of Bird claimed that she had been "appropriately circumspect, cautious, and thorough" in her review of all the cases, and she was joined by at least one other justice in overturning each sentence. Opponents of Bird and her death penalty decisions claimed that she used a "series of minute legal technicalities . . . to prevent the implementation of California's death penalty" as the only California Supreme Court jurist between 1978 (when California's death penalty statute went into effect) and 1986 who had not voted to affirm a single death penalty case.[37] Bird's opponents were eventually victorious, as California voters removed Bird and two of her liberal colleagues from the Court in a 2 to 1 vote in 1986. The election marked the first time that Californians had voted not to retain a Supreme Court justice. Bird died at the age of sixty-three from complications of breast cancer in 1999. Since leaving the high court, she had remained completely out of the spotlight. However, regardless of one's opinion on the death penalty, perhaps Bird's legacy can be found in the fact that California continues to have the largest backlog of death row inmates in the nation.

of ideology or party, tend to be stronger supporters of women's rights claims in cases than are men judges and that the presence of at least one woman on a bench (for example, an appeals court that hands down rulings with more than one judge participating) had a strong impact on the outcomes of sex-discrimination cases in favor of women.[38] The appointment of Sandra Day O'Connor in 1981 to the US Supreme Court shifted support toward women's rights; Ruth Bader Ginsburg's appointment in 1993 had a similar, if smaller, impact. The two women justices wrote half of the Court's majority opinions in the area of sex discrimination and often served as its spokespeople on women's rights issues.[39] Some feminist scholars have also looked for a different or feminist voice in legal decisions emanating from women judges. Little evidence exists to date that would show that placing women on the bench has altered modes of legal reasoning throughout the judiciary. Yet as women judges move beyond token status and increase their numbers on the bench, future research will likely reveal that "real changes in the law have been and will continue to be the result of the hard work done by women in the American judiciary."[40]

■ Conclusion

As is the case in other political institutions, women are just now starting to make an impact as judges at all levels of the judicial system. Although it may be too early to tell if women judges will dramatically change the processes and outcomes of judicial policymaking at either the state or national level, it is clear that women continue to enter the legal profession in record numbers and will no doubt continue to gain many more judicial positions in the coming years. According to Sandra Day O'Connor, she and Ruth Bader Ginsburg became important role models for other women aspiring to top leadership positions: "My intuition and my experience persuade me that having women on the bench, and in other positions of prominence, is extremely important. The self-perception of women is informed by such examples, and by the belief of women that they, too, can achieve professional success at the highest levels."[41]

The appointments of O'Connor and Ginsburg, according to Lawrence Baum, reflected "changes in society that made it at least somewhat less difficult for people other than white men to achieve high positions." And as we have seen, particularly with the confirmation of Sonia Sotomayor to the Supreme Court, presidents are now more willing to consider women and members of racial minority groups as judicial nominees. It is true that, "because of the various advantages they enjoy, white men are more likely to enjoy disproportionate representation on the Court for some time."[42] But male dominance over the legal profession is not nearly as strong as it once was as women continue to break down barriers to achieve positions of power and leadership within the federal and state judicial branches.

Study/Discussion Questions

1. What progress have women made in the legal profession since the latter part of the twentieth century? Why has it been so important for women entering judicial positions at both the state and federal level?

2. Why have there been so few presidential appointments of women to judicial positions at the federal level?

3. How have Supreme Court justices Sandra Day O'Connor and Ruth Bader Ginsburg made a difference for women in the legal profession?

4. What role have women played within state court systems in recent years?

5. How might women judges have an impact on public policies affecting women?

Online Resources

Federal Judges Biographical Database, Federal Judicial Center. http://www.fjc.gov/history/home.nsf.
National Association of Women Judges. http://www.nawj.org.
National Conference of Women's Bar Associations. http://www.ncwba.org.
Women's Legal History Biography Project. http://www.law.stanford.edu/library/wlhbp.

Notes

1. Oyez, "Biography of Sandra Day O'Connor."
2. Biskupic, "Ginsburg 'Lonely' Without O'Connor."
3. Mezey, *In Pursuit of Equality*, 8.

4. Ibid., 10–17; see also O'Brien, *Constitutional Law and Politics*, 1514–1516.

5. MacKinnon, "Women and Law," 447.

6. Commission on Women in the Profession, "A Current Glance at Women in the Law 2008."

7. Herring, "Can They Do It?" 76.

8. Rhode, "The Unfinished Agenda," 5.

9. Commission on Women in the Profession, "A Current Glance at Women in the Law 2008."

10. Rhode, "The Unfinished Agenda," 6.

11. Ibid., 7.

12. Ibid., 20.

13. Ibid., 20–22.

14. See Palmer, "Women in the American Judiciary."

15. Pacelle, "A President's Legacy," 154.

16. Rhode, "The Unfinished Agenda," 26.

17. Martin, "Bias or Counterbalance?" 255–256.

18. Baum, *The Supreme Court*, 35–47.

19. Ibid., 54–57.

20. O'Brien, *Storm Center*, 34–55.

21. Silverstein, *Judicious Choices*, 6.

22. See Baum, *The Supreme Court*, 38–40, and Silverstein, *Judicious Choices*, 213–217.

23. Baum, *The Supreme Court*, 34.

24. Abraham, *Justices, Presidents, and Senators*, 318.

25. Baum, *The Supreme Court*, 135.

26. Abraham, *Justices, Presidents, and Senators*, 322.

27. Hill, "What Difference Will Women Judges Make?" 183.

28. Lyles, *The Gatekeepers*, 262–263.

29. Pacelle, "A President's Legacy," 149.

30. O'Connor, *The Majesty of the Law*, 195.

31. Thomas, *How Women Legislate*, 18–20.

32. National Association of Women Judges, "Statistics."

33. Curran and Carson, *The Lawyer Statistical Report*.

34. Martin, "Bias or Counterbalance?" 283–284.

35. See Gruhl, Spohn, and Welch, "Women as Policymakers."

36. California Courts, "Chief Justice Rose Elizabeth Bird Dies."

37. Rose Bird ProCon, "The Death Penalty."

38. For example, see Davis, Haire, and Songer, "Voting Behavior and Gender on the U.S. Courts of Appeal"; Martin, "The Representative Role of Women Judges"; and Gryski, Main, and Dixon, "Models of State High Court Decision Making in Sex Discrimination Cases."

39. See Palmer, "Justice Ruth Bader Ginsburg and the Supreme Court's Reaction to Its Second Female Member."

40. See Palmer, "Women in the American Judiciary."

41. O'Connor, *The Majesty of the Law*, 189.

42. Baum, *The Supreme Court*, 58.

8

Women and Political Leadership in the Twenty-first Century

A woman will be president. Why? Because we're expert clean-ers and the world is a mess.
■ Marie Wilson, founder of the White House Project

The role of women in US public life presents both a long and complex story and a work in progress. For all the public policies changed, offices held, and barriers broken, many challenges remain for women political leaders on both ends of the political spectrum. As stated in Chapter 1, those with political power are those who hold specific leadership positions within government. And although we can imagine how different the political process might look and operate if more government officials were women, the reality remains that in the early years of the twenty-first century, women are still nowhere near holding even half the seats of power at all levels of the US government. Achieving that goal may be possible, but slower progress in the last few years in placing women into political leadership positions suggests that it will take longer than was optimistically claimed in 1992, "The Year of the Woman." In this concluding chapter, we briefly con-sider ongoing challenges for women within the political process as voters, candidates, and political officeholders. Returning to the theme of leadership, we also consider how women impact the political and policymaking process as leaders and what the future may hold.

■ **The Women's Movement**

As discussed in Chapter 2, the third wave of the women's movement has emerged and looks somewhat different than its predecessor, yet still represents some basic themes of feminism and legal equality. However, there is disagreement within feminist circles about what a third wave of the women's movement stands for or even if it truly exists. For the most part, the younger generation of feminist activists takes a more global and inclusive perspective than did their precedessors in the second wave of the women's movement, including a much wider range of views and issues. Perhaps the biggest challenge for the leaders of the third wave is simply the political environment in which they find themselves attempting to pursue certain policies. During the George W. Bush presidency, the focus of governmental resources on foreign policy issues related to terrorism and national security left little room either on the US policy agenda for women's concerns or in the national political dialogue for feminist voices to be heard. And since the definition of feminism and women's rights was more complex and broader than during the second wave of the women's movement, there was no clear consensus on which to build an agenda. In 2002, historian Barbara Epstein warned, "The wind has gone out of the sails, not only of the women's movement but also of the progressive movement as a whole in the United States generally. . . . Part of the answer is that feminism has become more an idea than a movement. And even as a movement, it lacks some of the impetus that it once had."[1]

Yet by 2008, the national agenda had changed quite dramatically, as the onset of a deep recession shifted the US dialogue from foreign policy and national security to economic and domestic matters. In addition, the political resurgence of the Democratic Party, which won control of Congress in 2006 and the White House in 2008, breathed new life into the progressive movement. In 2009, the Obama administration began to chart a much different policy course that included economic recovery, energy reform, and health care reform, among others. And in what served as an important substantive and symbolic victory for women's rights, the Lilly Ledbetter Fair Pay Act of 2009 became the first congressional bill signed into law by President Obama on January 29, 2009.

Nonetheless, legal reform within the US governing system is still seen by many women's rights activists as a top priority. Legal scholar Susan Gluck Mezey argues that legal reform can serve as an important vehicle for effecting societal change, and although the law by itself cannot end "political, social, and economic inequality, it sets a standard and creates a tone, in no small part because it responds to and helps engender awareness of feminist goals."[2] The fight for sex-based equality throughout the court system has in large part been a success for women's rights activists, who gained many new legal rights in the areas of work, education, and economics. However, pay inequity, the absence of women at higher levels of corporate and government leadership, attempts to restrict reproductive freedom, and a lack of effort to integrate family responsibilities into the workplace for both women and men are still important problems. As Mezey concludes, law and politics are "not perfect methods for transforming the United States into a more egalitarian society. Thus, despite important achievements in the law, society is not at the point where the differences between the sexes are interesting and intriguing but not determinative of a person's rights and stature."[3]

■ Voting Trends and the Gender Gap

Women make up more than half of the voting population in the United States and have the potential to make or break the candidates in any given election, and they have turned out in higher numbers than men in recent elections; they are often seen as "the crown jewel of the electorate."[4] But the gender gap has begun to narrow as women grow increasingly divided over key political issues. Given that women have never represented a monolithic voting bloc to begin with, that should not surprise any political observer. During the 2004 and 2008 presidential elections, the complexities of how women vote became even more apparent. The former showed there is a widening gulf between married women, who tend to vote Republican, and single women, who tend to vote Democratic. Democrats increased turnout among single women, while Republicans secured George W. Bush's reelection with the help of married women voters in strong Republican states in the Midwest and the South. However, in spite of the increasing marriage gap among both female and male voters, many political experts agree that the overall gender gap is "alive and well and cuts across marital, racial and age lines."[5] Also in 2004, Democrats fell short by their failure to rally women over their strongest issues, including health care and economic security, losing ground among white, working, and married women.

However, by 2008, the political fortunes of both parties had reversed, and women voters were suddenly being courted by two high-profile women candidates—Hillary Rodham Clinton in the Democratic primaries and Sarah Palin as the Republican vice presidential candidate during the general election. The political environment had changed as well, as voters prioritized economic and domestic issues (such as the housing crisis and the spiraling cost of health care) over foreign policy issues. And while Clinton put "18 million cracks" in the glass ceiling during her presidential campaign, Palin's vice presidential campaign prompted a new debate about feminism: could a socially conservative, prolife politician opposed to traditional women's rights issues such as fair pay legitimately call herself a feminist? Palin herself claimed to be a feminist during an interview with Katie Couric of CBS in September 2008 before stepping back from that statement a few weeks later by telling Brian Williams of NBC, "I'm not going to put a label on myself."[6] Women politicians of Palin's generation, whether Democrat or Republican, liberal or conservative, certainly benefited from the second wave of the women's movement in the 1960s and 1970s that opened up many more opportunities for women in politics, business, and all other aspects of public life. Yet Palin's emergence on the national scene in 2008 seemed to highlight what had been a growing competition in the political arena (as discussed in Chapter 2) between traditional feminist groups such as the National Organization for Women and antifeminist views supported by conservative women's groups such as the Independent Women's Forum.

The abortion issue also continues to play an important role in party politics, as each party continues to struggle to define its position on the divisive issue. During the past decade, the Republican Party has faced the challenge of contending with various factions within its ranks, including moderates (who may be fiscally conservative but socially moderate and prochoice, although the number of moderate Republicans holding public office continues to shrink), the old right (fiscal conservatives who favor small govern-

ment and are mostly prolife), and the new right (social conservatives who are staunchly prolife and support government intervention in areas involving morals and social values). After their electoral losses in 2004, the Democrats began debating whether to
distance themselves from their longtime prochoice stance because
of the Republican Party's success with voters on issues such as family and morality. And, at the start of the 109th Congress in 2005,
Democrats selected a new Senate minority leader, Harry Reid of
Nevada, who is Mormon and prolife. Just a few years prior, a prolife politician in a top leadership position within the Democratic
Party was unheard of; as recently as 1992, the party refused to
allow William Casey, then Democratic governor of Pennsylvania, a
speaking role at the Democratic National Convention due to his
prolife stance. But some within the Democratic Party saw Reid's
ascension to Senate minority leader (he would become Senate
majority leader in 2007) as a moderating move to tone down the
abortion rhetoric so as not to alienate middle-of-the-road voters.
The issue of abortion remained somewhat low-key during the
2008 presidential campaign, with a traditional matchup of a prochoice Democrat (Barack Obama) and a prolife Republican (John
McCain). In 2009, a Gallup poll showed that for the first time
since Gallup began asking the question in 1995, a majority of
Americans called themselves prolife (51 percent) rather than prochoice (42 percent).[7] How this issue will continue to play out in the
political arena in regard to women voters remains to be seen, yet
both parties seem committed in their attempts to increase voter
registration and turnout among women.

■ Women as Candidates

As discussed in Chapter 4, in spite of the progress that women
candidates have made in the area of campaign finance and the
ability to raise adequate funds to run a successful campaign, many
barriers remain to keep them from running for and getting elected
to public office. The power of incumbency presents the biggest
challenge, since incumbents, who are mostly men, have such a
large advantage over challengers, casting women as the "other" in
the electoral arena. Moreover, women candidates need more
encouragement to run, not only from individual supporters but

from parties and interest groups as well. Making the decision to run for political office is often the largest hurdle for a woman candidate to overcome. Although public opinion polls show that US voters largely support women as active participants in the political process and as candidates, studies also suggest that many women still believe that they would have a difficult time winning an election. This may be due to continuing stereotypes of women candidates and the emphasis on difference that they represent. According to political scientist Kathleen Dolan, "We still, in journalistic, popular, and academic accounts of their activities, refer to them as 'women candidates.' That we modify the noun 'candidates' in this way indicates that candidate sex is still a relevant, or at least obvious, aspect of their electoral activities."[8]

We do know that women voters do not automatically vote for women candidates, and that party identification as well as incumbency can play a much larger role than the sex of the candidate in terms of voter preference.[9] However, the number of women seeking elective office has leveled off in recent years, with fewer women running for state legislative positions in 2004. Since such political experience is often an important qualification for seeking higher political office, such as state governor or member of Congress, the decline in the number of women seeking state-level legislative positions is not a positive trend. The recruitment of women into political careers, as well as breaking down pervasive stereotypes about women candidates, is more important than ever, since many political observers believe that the emphasis on national security issues since September 11, 2001, and "continued perceptions among some voters as well as some potential female candidates that women should be caring for their families have limited participation."[10] As discussed in Chapter 6, the historic nature of both the Clinton and Palin campaigns in 2008 represents significant progress in moving away from the idea that a woman candidate for high office is an anomaly. Yet the true legacy of 2008 in terms of the breakdown of barriers for future women candidates for president and vice president has yet to be determined.

■ Women as Officeholders

Several studies show that women officeholders, especially in Congress and state legislatures, do make a difference in policy outcomes, particularly those directly affecting women.[11] At the start of 2009, a total of seventeen women were members of the US Senate. Although the number may still be low, several of these women on both sides of the political aisle are high-profile politicians who have gained tremendous ground in terms of seniority and committee assignments, including Barbara Mikulski (D-MD), Dianne Feinstein (D-CA), Barbara Boxer (D-CA), Olympia Snowe (R-ME), and Kay Bailey Hutchison (R-TX).

In the House of Representatives, the Congressional Caucus for Women's Issues continues to face challenges, including the recruitment of reliable cochairs from each party (self-styled Republican feminists are sometimes hard to recruit as it is difficult for them to commit to the agenda); the recruitment of enough reliable and committed members from each party; the maintenance of an organizational structure that promotes the agenda (holding regular meetings and reaching consensus among the growing membership has become more difficult in the absence of staff); the ability to set an agenda that is streamlined toward obtainable goals; the ability to adapt in the face of competing claims for national resources (the increased attention on terrorism, national security, and military/defense funding since September 11 has made budgeting for women's issues more challenging); and connecting with the White House and congressional leaders (the caucus's relationship with the Bush administration was distant, as women's/feminist issues were not prioritized on the conservative/Republican agenda, but with a Democratic Congress and Obama in the White House, relations are improving). As congressional scholar Irwin Gertzog argues, the caucus "is among the more long-lived informal groups in the House. Its robust size, its elastic agenda, its faithful membership, and its attentive constituency suggest that the organization will probably carry on for a while."[12]

The question also remains as to when a woman will be elected president or vice president. Public opinion polls still show support among voters for a woman to be elected president, yet there seems to be a continuing disconnect between that sentiment and the reality of presidential electoral politics. The US system of presidential nominations is often a contest of the "survival of the fittest" in terms of money, party support, name recognition, and a positive public image. Building on the Clinton and Palin campaigns in 2008, are there any viable women contenders for the White House in 2012 and/or 2016? Among Democrats, women candidates are being talked about for 2016, since it is not likely that a candidate will emerge to challenge President Obama in the Democratic primaries in 2012 (the last significant challenge to an incumbent president from within his own party came in 1980, when Senator Edward Kennedy beat President Jimmy Carter in several primaries before Carter finally won the nomination). Although no list is definitive, the names of several prominent women politicians often emerge as potential candidates, as we saw in Chapter 6; they include Health and Human Services Secretary (and former Kansas governor) Kathleen Sebelius (D), former New Jersey governor and former head of the Environmental Protection Agency Christine Todd Whitman (R), Connecticut governor Jodi Rell (R), Alaska senator Lisa Murkowski (R), and Florida congresswoman Debbie Wasserman Shultz (D).

Regardless of when the political glass ceiling is broken at the national level, both political parties must recognize that all women politicians, whether legislators or governors, bring a unique perspective to government and policymaking. What political scientist Kim Fridkin Kahn pointed out more than a decade ago is still true today: that "by limiting the number of women in elective office, we limit the attention of the government to predominantly male concerns and ignore the concerns of women and women legislators. A governing body that neglects a range of issues not only ignores the concerns of a large segment of the electorate but also may be less effective than a government addressing a wider spectrum of policy concerns."[13]

■ Conclusion: Women and Leadership Revisited

As this book illustrates, there is no universal definition of leadership, particularly for women in the political arena. Defining successful leadership is an elusive task, and debates about the role that sex and gender play in notions of leadership and about the difference that they can make in the political process will continue. According to political scientist Sue Thomas, "leadership can be exerted in a wide variety of ways, informally and formally, and in multiple milieus." The fact that leadership may also be a gendered concept has "implications for the possibilities and constraints on women in both achieving leadership positions and [in

determining] the ways they act once those positions are gained."
As a result, she suggests that future academic studies of women
and political leadership should move beyond the narrow focus on
those who hold formal positions of political power to include
women of varying racial/ethnic and socioeconomic backgrounds
who are active political participants, as well as leaders in the political process in formal positions, appointed as well as elected, at all
levels of government; in other political positions such as lobbying
groups and administrative staffs; and informal (civic, community,
business, and clerical) positions.[14] If we expand our view of how
women can alter policy outcomes in a variety of leadership positions, we will have a better understanding of the role of women in
our society, past, present, and future.

Women in the United States have made much progress as
political leaders since the Seneca Falls Convention in 1848, yet
much work remains in the twenty-first century. Whether in the
political and legal arenas, the corporate world, higher education,
or any number of important civic or social roles, women leaders
can bring different perspectives to public life and can continue to
break down negative gender stereotypes. Many barriers to equality for women have been removed by the election and appointment
of women to high-ranking political positions. And more women
will have access to these positions of power as our society continues to accept and embrace women as political leaders. Women,
when viewed as an inclusive group, represent political perspectives, policy choices, and backgrounds that run the gamut of partisan and ideological preferences. However, if the level of political
participation of its citizens defines the level of democracy within a
government, then the continued increase of all women as active
political participants will help to ensure that the democratic ideal
of our system of government endures.

■ **Study/Discussion Questions**

1. What are some of the challenges that the women's movement will face in the next decade? Will the third wave of the
women's movement be successful?

2. Will the gender gap in voting continue, and what are the
prospects for increasing voter turnout among women?

3. What are the biggest challenges that women candidates continue to face in the electoral arena? What are some suggestions for increasing the number of women running for public office?

4. Will women ever reach parity with men in terms of elected and appointed political positions at the state and national levels?

■ **Notes**

1. Epstein, "The Successes and Failures of Feminism," 118.
2. Mezey, *Elusive Equality*, 3.
3. Ibid., 288.
4. Clift, "Capitol Letter: The Gender Gap."
5. Sweet, "Did the Women's Vote Count?" 60.
6. CNN, "Palin Changes Tune on Feminist Label."
7. Gallup, "More Americans 'Pro-Life' Than 'Pro-Choice' for First Time."
8. Dolan, *Voting for Women*, 153.
9. Ibid., 156.
10. Milligan, "Regression After Year of the Woman," A14.
11. See Caiazza, "Does Women's Representation in Elected Office Lead to Women-Friendly Policy?"
12. Gertzog, *Women and Power on Capitol Hill*, 161.
13. Kahn, *The Political Consequences of Being a Woman*, 138.
14. Thomas, "The Impact of Women in Political Leadership Positions," 89–90.

Bibliography

Abraham, Henry J. *Justices, Presidents, and Senators: A History of the U.S. Supreme Court Appointments from Washington to Clinton.* Lanham, MD: Rowman and Littlefield, 1999.

Abramowitz, Alan. *Voice of the People: Elections and Voting in the United States.* New York: McGraw-Hill, 2004.

Arneil, Barbara. *Politics and Feminism.* Oxford, UK: Blackwell Publishers, 1999.

Baer, Denise L. "Women, Women's Organizations, and Political Parties," in *Women and American Politics: New Questions, New Directions,* ed. Susan J. Carroll. New York: Oxford University Press, 2003.

Baer, Judith A. *Our Lives Before the Law: Constructing a Feminist Jurisprudence.* Princeton, NJ: Princeton University Press, 1999.

Baird, Julia. "From Seneca Falls to . . . Sarah Palin?" *Newsweek,* September 13, 2008. http://www.newsweek.com/id/158893/page/1.

Banner, Lois W. "Elizabeth Cady Stanton," in *The Oxford Companion to United States History,* ed. Paul S. Boyer. New York: Oxford University Press, 2001.

Barnett, Rosalind Chait. "Women, Leadership, and the Natural Order," in *Women and Leadership: The State of Play and Strategies for Change,* eds. Barbara Kellerman and Deborah L. Rhode. New York: Wiley, 2007, 154–156.

Barth, Jay, and Margaret R. Ferguson. "Gender and Gubernatorial Personality." *Women and Politics* 24, no. 1 (2002): 63–82.

Baum, Lawrence. *The Supreme Court,* 9th ed. Washington, DC: CQ Press, 2007.

Baumgardner, Jennifer, and Amy Richards. *Manifesta: Young Women, Feminism, and the Future.* New York: Farrar, Straus and Giroux, 2000.

Bergmann, Barbara R. *The Economic Emergence of Women,* 2nd ed. New York: Palgrave Macmillan, 2005.

Biskupic, Joan. "Ginsburg 'Lonely' Without O'Connor." *USA Today*, December 5, 2007. http://www.usatoday.com/news/washington/2007-01-25-ginsburg-court_x.htm.

Blyth, Myrna. *Spin Sisters: How the Women of the Media Sell Unhappiness—and Liberalism—to the Women of America*. New York: St. Martin's Press, 2004.

Book, Esther Wachs. *Why the Best Man for the Job Is a Woman: The Unique Female Qualities of Leadership*. New York: HarperCollins, 2000.

Borrelli, MaryAnne. "The First Lady as Formal Advisor to the President: When East (Wing) Meets West (Wing)." *Women and Politics* 24, no. 1 (2002): 25–45.

———. *The President's Cabinet: Gender, Power, and Representation*. Boulder, CO: Lynne Rienner, 2002.

Borrelli, MaryAnne, and Janet M. Martin, eds. *The Other Elites: Women, Politics, and Power in the Executive Branch*. Boulder, CO: Lynne Rienner, 1997.

Bourque, Susan C. "Political Leadership for Women: Redefining Power and Reassessing the Political," in *Women on Power: Leadership Redefined*, eds. Sue J.M. Freeman, Susan C. Bourque, and Christine M. Shelton. Boston: Northeastern University Press, 2001.

Braden, Maria. *Women Politicians and the Media*. Lexington: University Press of Kentucky, 1996.

Burns, James MacGregor. *Leadership*. New York: Harper and Row, 1978.

———. *Transforming Leadership*. New York: Atlantic Monthly Press, 2003.

Burrell, Barbara. "Campaign Finance: Women's Experience in the Modern Era," in *Women and Elective Office: Past, Present, and Future*, eds. Sue Thomas and Clyde Wilcox. New York: Oxford University Press, 1998, 26–40.

———. "Money and Women's Candidacies for Public Office," in Susan J. Carroll, ed., *Women and American Politics: New Questions, New Direcitons*. New York: Oxford University Press, 2003.

———. "The Office of the First Lady and Public Policymaking," in *The Other Elites: Women, Politics, and Power in the Executive Branch*, eds. MaryAnne Borrelli and Janet M. Martin. Boulder, CO: Lynne Rienner, 1997.

Bystrom, Dianne. "On the Way to the White House: Communication Strategies for Women Candidates," in *Anticipating Madam President*, eds. Robert P. Watson and Ann Gordon. Boulder, CO: Lynne Rienner Publishers, 2003.

Bystrom, Dianne G., Mary Christine Banwart, Lynda Lee Kaid, and Terry A. Robertson. *Gender and Candidate Communication: VideoStyle, WebStyle, NewsStyle*. New York: Routledge, 2004.

Caiazza, Amy. "Does Women's Representation in Elected Office Lead to Women-Friendly Policy? Analysis of State-Level Data." *Women and Politics* 26, no. 1 (2004): 35–65.

California Courts. "Chief Justice Rose Elizabeth Bird Dies; Supreme

Court to Hold Memorial Session." News release of the California Supreme Court, December 6, 1999, no. 78. http://www.courtinfo.ca .gov/presscenter/newsreleases/NR78-99.htm.

Carey, John M., Richard G. Niemi, and Lynda W. Powell. "Are Women Legislators Different?" in *Women and Elective Office: Past, Present, and Future*, eds. Sue Thomas and Clyde Wilcox. New York: Oxford University Press, 1998.

Carli, Linda L., and Alice H. Eagly. "Overcoming Resistance to Women Leaders: The Importance of Leadership Style," in *Women and Leadership: The State of Play and Strategies for Change*, eds. Barbara Kellerman and Deborah L. Rhode. New York: Wiley, 2007.

Carroll, Susan J. "Representing Women: Congresswomen's Perceptions of Their Representational Roles," in *Women Transforming Congress*, ed. Cindy Simon Rosenthal. Norman: University of Oklahoma Press, 2002.

———. "Representing Women: Women State Legislators as Agents of Policy-Related Change," in *The Impact of Women in Public Office*, ed. Susan J. Carroll. Bloomington: Indiana University Press, 2001, 17–18.

———, ed. *Women and American Politics: New Questions, New Directions.* New York: Oxford University Press, 2003.

———. *Women as Candidates in American Politics*, 2nd ed. Bloomington: Indiana University Press, 1994.

———. "Women in State Government: Historical Overview and Current Trends." Center for American Women and Politics. http://www .cawp.rutgers.edu/research/reports/BookofStates.pdf.

———. "Women Voters and the Gender Gap." American Political Science Association. http://www.apsanet.org/print/printer_ content_5270.cfm.

Carroll, Susan J., and Linda M. G. Zerilli. "Feminist Challenges to Political Science," in *Political Science: The State of the Discipline II*, ed. Ada W. Finifter. Washington, DC: American Political Science Association, 1993, 55–72.

CBS News. "Ready for a Woman President?" CBS News, February 5, 2006. www.cbsnews.com.

Center for American Women and Politics. "Fast Facts: Congress," Center for American Women and Politics, Eagleton Institute of Politics, Rutgers, The State University of New Jersey. http://www .cawp.rutgers.edu/fast_facts/levels_of_office/congress.php.

———. "The Gender Gap." Center for American Women and Politics, Eagleton Institute of Politics, Rutgers, The State University of New Jersey. http://www.cawp.rutgers.edu/fast_facts/voters/documents/ GGPresVote.pdf.

———. "Statewide Elective Executive Women 2009." Eagleton Institute of Politics, Rutgers, The State University of New Jersey. http:// www.cawp.rutgers.edu/fast_facts/levels_of_office/documents/stwide .pdf.

———. "Women in State Legislatures 2009." Center for American

Women and Politics, Eagleton Institute of Politics, Rutgers, The State University of New Jersey. http://www.cawp.rutgers.edu/fast _facts/levels_of_office/documents/stleg.pdf.

———. "Women State Legislators: Leadership Positions and Committee Chairs 2007." Center for American Women and Politics, Eagleton Institute of Politics, Rutgers, The State University of New Jersey. http://www.cawp.rutgers.edu/fast_facts/levels_of_office/documents/ Leglead07.pdf.

"The Changing Face of Orange County," *California Journal*, June 1, 2001. http://www.statenet.com/capital-journal.

Clift, Eleanor. "Capitol Letter: The Gender Gap." *Newsweek*, May 14, 2004. http://www.newsweek.com/id/105048.

Clift, Eleanor, and Tom Brazaitis. *Madam President: Shattering the Last Glass Ceiling*. New York: Scribner, 2000.

Clinton, Hillary Rodham. *Living History*. New York: Simon and Schuster, 2003.

CNN. "Palin Changes Tune on Feminist Label." CNN, October 23, 2008. http://politicalticker.blogs.cnn.com/2008/10/23/palin-changes -tune-on-feminist-label/?eref=politicalflipper.

Cobble, Dorothy Sue, ed. *The Sex of Class: Women Transforming American Labor*. Ithaca, NY: IRL Press, 2007.

Collins, Patricia Hill. *Black Feminist Thought: Knowledge, Consciousness, and the Politics of Empowerment*. Boston: Unwin Hyman, 1990.

Commission on Women in the Profession. "A Current Glance at Women in the Law 2008." Commission on Women in the Profession, American Bar Association. http://www.abanet.org/women/Current GlanceStatistics2008.pdf.

"Convention Notebook: During Drafty Delay in a Garage, Protocol Rules It's Ladies First." *Los Angeles Times*, July 20, 1984, A7.

Conway, M. Margaret, David W. Ahern, and Gertrude A. Steuernagel. *Women and Political Participation: Cultural Change in the Political Arena*. Washington, DC: CQ Press, 1997.

———. *Women and Public Policy: A Revolution in Progress*, 3rd ed. Washington, DC: CQ Press, 2005.

Cook, Elizabeth Adell. "Voter Reaction to Women Candidates," in *Women and Elective Office: Past, Present, and Future*, eds. Sue Thomas and Clyde Wilcox. New York: Oxford University Press, 1998.

Costain, Anne N. "Paving the Way: The Work of the Women's Movement," in *Anticipating Madam President*, eds. Robert P. Watson and Ann Gordon. Boulder, CO: Lynne Rienner Publishers, 2003, 31–42.

Cronin, Thomas E., and Michael A. Genovese. *The Paradoxes of the American Presidency*. New York: Oxford University Press, 1998.

Curran, Barbara A., and Clara N. Carson. *The Lawyer Statistical Report: The U.S. Legal Profession in the 1990s*. Chicago: American Bar Foundation, 1994.

Darcy, R., Susan Welch, and Janet Clark. *Women, Elections, and Representation*. Lincoln: University of Nebraska Press, 1994.

Davis, Sue, Susan Haire, and Donald Songer. "Voting Behavior and Gender on the U.S. Courts of Appeal." *Judicature* 77 (1993): 129–133.

Day, Christine L., and Charles D. Hadley. *Women's PACs: Abortion and Elections*. Upper Saddle River, NJ: Pearson/Prentice Hall, 2005.

DeConde, Alexander. *Presidential Machismo: Executive Authority, Military Intervention, and Foreign Relations*. Boston: Northeastern University Press, 2000.

Deemer, Candy, and Nancy Fredericks. *Dancing on the Glass Ceiling*. Chicago: Contemporary Books, 2003.

Denes, Melissa. "Feminism? It's Hardly Begun." *The Guardian*, January 17, 2005. http://www.guardian.co.uk/g2/story/0,3604,1391841,00.html.

Dolan, Kathleen A. *Voting for Women: How the Public Evaluates Women Candidates*. Boulder, CO: Westview Press, 2004.

DuBois, Ellen C. "Susan B. Anthony," in *The Oxford Companion to United States History*, ed. Paul S. Boyer. New York: Oxford University Press, 2001.

Duerst-Lahti, Georgia. "The Bottleneck: Women Becoming Candidates," in *Women and Elective Office: Past, Present, and Future*, eds. Sue Thomas and Clyde Wilcox. New York: Oxford University Press, 1998.

———. "Reconceiving Theories of Power: Consequences of Masculinism in the Executive Branch," in *The Other Elites: Women, Politics, and Power in the Executive Branch*, eds. MaryAnne Borrelli and Janet M. Martin. Boulder, CO: Lynne Rienner, 1997.

Dye, Thomas R. *Who's Running America? The Bush Restoration*, 7th ed. Upper Saddle River, NJ: Prentice Hall, 2002.

Eagly, Alice H., and Mary C. Johannesen-Schmidt. "The Leadership Styles of Women and Men." *Journal of Social Sciences* 57, no. 4 (2001): 781–797.

Elder, Laurel. "Why Women Don't Run: Explaining Women's Underrepresentation in America's Political Institutions." *Women and Politics* 26, no. 2 (2004): 27–56.

Ellison, Sheila. *If Women Ruled the World: How to Create the World We Want to Live In*. Novato, CA: New World Library, 2004.

Epstein, Barbara. "The Successes and Failures of Feminism." *Journal of Women's History* 14, no. 2 (2002): 118–125.

Epstein, Laurily Keir, ed. *Women and the News*. New York: Hastings House, 1978.

Epstein, Lee, and Thomas G. Walker. *Constitutional Law for a Changing America: A Short Course*, 4th ed. Washington, DC: CQ Press, 2009.

Epstein, Michael J., Richard G. Niemi, and Lynda W. Powell. "Do Women and Men State Legislators Differ?" in *Women and Elective Office: Past, Present, and Future*, eds. Sue Thomas and Clyde Wilcox. New York: Oxford University Press, 1998, 94–109.

Evans, Sara M. *Tidal Wave: How Women Changed America at Century's End*. New York: Free Press, 2003.

Falk, Erika, and Kathleen Hall Jamieson. "Changing the Climate of Expectations," in *Anticipating Madam President*, eds. Robert P. Watson and Ann Gordon. Boulder, CO: Lynne Rienner Publishers, 2003, 43–52.

Farber, Jim. "Geraldine Ferraro Lets Her Emotions Do the Talking." *Daily Breeze*, March 7, 2008.

Farrar-Myers, Victoria A. "A War Chest Full of Susan B. Anthony Dollars: Fund-raising Issues for Female Presidential Candidates," in *Anticipating Madam President*, eds. Robert P. Watson and Ann Gordon. Boulder, CO: Lynne Rienner Publishers, 2003, 81–94.

Ferguson, Michaele L., and Lori Jo Marso, eds. *W Stands for Women: How the George W. Bush Presidency Shaped a New Politics of Gender*. Durham, NC: Duke University Press, 2007.

Ferraro, Geraldine A., and Linda Francke. *Ferraro: My Story*. New York: Bantam Books, 1985.

Findlen, Barbara, ed. *Listen Up: Voices from the Next Feminist Generation*. Seattle: Seal Press, 1995.

Ford, Lynne E. *Women and Politics: The Pursuit of Equality*, 2nd ed. Boston: Wadsworth, 2005.

Ford, Lynne E., and Kathleen Dolan. "Women State Legislators: Three Decades of Gains in Representation and Diversity," in *Women in Politics: Outsiders or Insiders?* 3rd ed., ed. Lois Duke Whitaker. Upper Saddle River, NJ: Prentice Hall, 1999.

Fox, Richard L. "The Future of Women's Political Leadership: Gender and the Decision to Run for Elective Office," in *Women and Leadership: The State of Play and Strategies for Change*, eds. Barbara Kellerman and Deborah L. Rhode. New York: Wiley, 2007, 251–270.

Fox, Richard L., and Jennifer L. Lawless. "Entering the Arena? Gender and the Decision to Run for Office." *American Journal of Political Science* 48, no. 2 (2004): 264–280.

Francia, Peter L. "Early Fundraising by Nonincumbent Female Congressional Candidates: The Importance of Women's PACs." *Women and Politics* 23, no. 1/2 (2001): 7–20.

Freeman, Jo. *A Room at a Time: How Women Entered Party Politics*. Lanham, MD: Rowman & Littlefield, 2000.

———. *We Will Be Heard: Women's Struggles for Political Power in the United States*. Lanham, MD: Rowman and Littlefield, 2008.

Freeman, Sue J.M., and Susan C. Bourque. "Leadership and Power: New Conceptions," in *Women on Power: Leadership Redefined*, eds. Sue J.M. Freeman, Susan C. Bourque, and Christine M. Shelton. Boston: Northeastern University Press, 2001.

Freeman, Sue J.M., Susan C. Bourque, and Christine M. Shelton, eds. *Women on Power: Leadership Redefined*. Boston: Northeastern University Press, 2001.

Friedan, Betty. *The Feminine Mystique*. New York: W. W. Norton, 2001.

———. *It Changed My Life: Writings on the Women's Movement*. New York: Random House, 1978.

Gallup. "More Americans 'Pro-Life' Than 'Pro-Choice' for First Time."
   Gallup, May 15, 2009. http://www.gallup.com/poll/118399/
   More-Americans-Pro-Life-Than-Pro-Choice- First-Time.aspx.
Gandy, Kim. "The *New York Times*' Woman Problem," National
   Organization for Women Political Action Site, September 14, 2003.
   http://www.nowpacs.org/2004/letter.html.
García, Alma M. "The Development of Chicana Feminist Discourse,
   1980." *Gender and Society* 3, no. 2 (1989): 217–238.
Genovese, Michael A., ed. *Women as National Leaders.* Thousand Oaks,
   CA: Sage, 1993.
———. "Women as National Leaders: What Do We Know?" in *Women
   as National Leaders,* ed. Michael A. Genovese. Thousand Oaks, CA:
   Sage, 1993.
Gertzog, Irwin N. *Congressional Women: Their Recruitment, Integration,
   and Behavior,* 2nd ed. Westport, CT: Praeger, 1995.
———. *Women and Power on Capitol Hill.* Boulder, CO: Lynne Rienner
   Publishers, 2004.
Goldstein, Leslie Friedman, ed. *Feminist Jurisprudence: The Difference
   Debate.* Lanham, MD: Rowman and Littlefield, 1992.
Graber, Doris A. *Mass Media and American Politics,* 7th ed. Washington,
   DC: CQ Press, 2006.
Graham, Katherine. *Personal History.* New York: Knopf, 1997.
Green, Joshua. "The Front-Runner's Fall." *The Atlantic,* September
   2008.
Greenstein, Fred I. "George W. Bush and the Ghosts of Presidents
   Past." *PS: Political Science and Politics* 34, no. 1 (2001): 77–80.
Gruhl, John, Cassis Spohn, and Susan Welch. "Women as Policymakers:
   The Case of Trial Judges." *American Journal of Political Science* 25,
   no. 2 (1981): 308–322.
Gryski, Gerard, Eleanor Main, and William Dixon. "Models of State
   High Court Decision Making in Sex Discrimination Cases." *Journal
   of Politics* 48 (1986): 143–155.
Hall, Cynthia A. "The Congressional Caucus for Women's Issues at 25:
   Challenges and Opportunities," in *The American Woman 2003–2004:
   Daughters of a Revolution—Young Women Today,* eds. Cynthia B.
   Costello, Vanessa R. Wight, and Anne J. Stone. New York: Palgrave
   Macmillan, 2003.
Han, Lori Cox. "Presidential Leadership: Governance from a Woman's
   Perspective," in *Anticipating Madam President,* eds. Robert P. Watson
   and Ann Gordon. Boulder, CO: Lynne Rienner Publishers, 2003,
   163–176.
Han, Lori Cox, and Caroline Heldman, eds. *Rethinking Madam President:
   Are We Ready for a Woman in the White House?* Boulder, CO: Lynne
   Rienner Publishers, 2007.
Harper, Judith E. "Biography of Susan B. Anthony and Elizabeth Cady
   Stanton." PBS. http://www.pbs.org/stantonanthony/resources/index
   .html.

Hearn, Josephine. "Sanchez Accuses Democrat of Calling Her a 'Whore,' Resigns From Hispanic Group," Politico, January 31, 2007. http://www.politico.com/news/stories/0107/2572.html.

Heith, Diane J. "The Lipstick Watch: Media Coverage, Gender, and Presidential Campaigns," in *Anticipating Madam President*, eds. Robert P. Watson and Ann Gordon. Boulder, CO: Lynne Rienner Publishers, 2003, 123–130.

Heldman, Caroline, Susan J. Carroll, and Stephanie Olson. "'She Brought Only a Skirt': Print Media Coverage of Elizabeth Dole's Bid for the Republican Nomination." *Political Communication* 22 (2005): 315–335.

Helgesen, Sally. *The Female Advantage: Women's Ways of Leadership*. New York: Doubleday, 1990.

Henry, Astrid. *Not My Mother's Sister*. Bloomington: Indiana University Press, 2004.

Herring, Jacob A. "Can They Do It? Can Law Firms, Corporate Counsel Departments, and Governmental Agencies Create a Level Playing Field for Women Attorneys?" in *The Difference "Difference" Makes: Women and Leadership*, ed. Deborah L. Rhode. Stanford, CA: Stanford University Press, 2003.

Hill, Anita F. "What Difference Will Women Judges Make?" in *Women and Leadership: The State of Play and Strategies for Change*, eds. Barbara Kellerman and Deborah L. Rhode. New York: Wiley, 2007.

Holvino, Evangelina. "Women and Power: New Perspectives on Old Challenges," in *Women and Leadership: The State of Play and Strategies for Change*, eds. Barbara Kellerman and Deborah L. Rhode. New York: Wiley, 2007.

Hoyt, Crystal L. "Women and Leadership," in *Leadership: Theory and Practice*, 4th ed., ed. Peter G. Northouse. Thousand Oaks, CA: Sage, 2006.

Huddy, Leonie, and Nayda Terkildsen. "Gender Stereotypes and the Perception of Male and Female Candidates." *American Journal of Political Science* 37 (1993): 119–147.

Infoplease. "Geraldine Anne Ferraro." Infoplease. http://www.infoplease.com/ce6/people/A0818528.html.

"The Invisible Primary—Invisible No Longer: A First Look at Coverage of the 2008 Presidential Campaign," Project for Excellence in Journalism and the Joan Shorenstein Center, Harvard University, October 29, 2007. http://www.journalism.org.node/8187.

Jamieson, Kathleen Hall. *Beyond the Double Bind: Women and Leadership*. New York: Oxford University Press, 1995.

Jeydel, Alana S. *Political Women: The Women's Movement, Political Institutions, the Battle for Women's Suffrage and the ERA*. New York: Routledge, 2004.

Kahn, Kim Fridkin. "Assessing the Media's Impact on the Political Fortunes of Women," in *Women and American Politics: New Questions, New Directions*, ed. Susan J. Carroll. New York: Oxford University Press, 2003.

———. *The Political Consequences of Being a Woman*. New York: Columbia University Press, 1996.

Kantor, Jodi. "Where the Votes Are, So, Unfortunately, Are All Those Calories." *New York Times*, November 23, 2007, A1.

Kellerman, Barbara. "You've Come a Long Way, Baby—and You've Got Miles to Go," in *The Difference "Difference" Makes: Women and Leadership*, ed. Deborah L. Rhode. Stanford, CA: Stanford University Press, 2003.

Kellerman, Barbara, and Deborah L. Rhode, eds. *Women and Leadership: The State of Play and Strategies for Change*. New York: Wiley, 2007.

Kenski, Kate, and Erika Falk. "Of What Is This Glass Ceiling Made? A Study of Attitudes About Women and the Oval Office." *Women and Politics* 26, no. 2 (2004): 57–80.

Klenke, Karin. *Women and Leadership: A Contextual Perspective*. New York: Springer Publishing, 1996.

Kolmar, Wendy K., and Frances Bartkowski. *Feminist Theory: A Reader*, 2nd ed. New York: McGraw-Hill, 2005.

Kropf, Martha E., and John A. Boiney. "The Electoral Glass Ceiling? Gender, Viability, and the News in U.S. Senate Campaigns." *Women and Politics* 23, no. 1/2 (2001): 79–101.

Lawless, Jennifer L., and Richard L. Fox. *It Takes a Candidate: Why Women Don't Run for Office*. New York: Cambridge University Press, 2005.

Lawless, Jennifer L., and Kathryn Pearson. "The Primary Reason for Women's Underrepresentation? Reevaluating the Conventional Wisdom." *The Journal of Politics* 70, no. 1 (2008): 67–82.

Levin, Phyllis Lee. *Abigail Adams: A Biography*. New York: St. Martin's Press, 1987.

Lyles, Kevin. *The Gatekeepers: Federal District Courts in the Political Process*. Westport, CT: Praeger, 1997.

MacKinnon, Catharine A. "Women and Law: The Power to Change," in *Sisterhood Is Forever: The Women's Anthology for a New Millennium*, ed. Robin Morgan. New York: Washington Square Press, 2003.

Mandel, Ruth B. "A Question About Women and the Leadership Option," in *The Difference "Difference" Makes: Women and Leadership*, ed. Deborah L. Rhode. Stanford, CA: Stanford University Press, 2003.

Mann, James. *Rise of the Vulcans: The History of Bush's War Cabinet*. New York: Viking Press, 2004.

Mansbridge, Jane J. *Why We Lost the ERA*. Chicago: University of Chicago Press, 1986.

Marks, Alexandra. "The Quest of Carol Moseley Braun." *The Christian Science Monitor*, November 19, 2003, 1.

Marshall, Brenda DeVore, and Molly A. Mayhead. "The Changing Face of the Governorship," in *Navigating Boundaries: The Rhetoric of Women Governors*, eds. Brenda DeVore Marshall and Molly A. Mayhead. Westport, CT: Praeger, 2000.

———, eds. *Navigating Boundaries: The Rhetoric of Women Governors*. Westport, CT: Praeger, 2000.

Martin, Elaine. "Bias or Counterbalance?: Women Judges Making a Difference," in *Women in Politics: Outsiders or Insiders?* 4th ed., ed. Lois Duke Whitaker. Upper Saddle River, NJ: Prentice Hall, 2006.

———. "The Representative Role of Women Judges." *Judicature* 77 (1993): 166–173.

Martin, Janet M. *The Presidency and Women: Promise, Performance and Illusion.* College Station: Texas A&M University Press, 2003.

Matthews, Jean V. *Women's Struggle for Equality: The First Phase, 1828–1876.* Chicago: Ivan R. Dee, 1997.

McGlen, Nancy E., Karen O'Connor, Laura van Assendelft, and Wendy Gunther-Canada. *Women, Politics, and American Society,* 4th ed. New York: Longman, 2002.

Media Awareness Network. "Media Portrayals of Girls and Women," Media Awareness Network. http://www.media-awareness.ca/english/issues/stereotyping/women_and_girls/index.cfm.

Mezey, Susan Gluck. *Elusive Equality: Women's Rights, Public Policy, and the Law.* Boulder, CO: Lynne Rienner Publishers, 2003.

———. *In Pursuit of Equality: Women, Public Policy, and the Federal Courts.* New York: St. Martin's Press, 1992.

Michaels, Debra. "Stealth Feminists: The Thirtysomething Revolution," in *Sisterhood Is Forever: The Women's Anthology for a New Millennium,* ed. Robin Morgan. New York: Washington Square Press, 2003.

Milligan, Susan. "Regression After Year of the Woman." *Boston Globe,* January 30, 2005, A14.

Mills, Kay. "What Difference Do Women Journalists Make?" in *Women, Media, and Politics,* ed. Pippa Norris. New York: Oxford University Press, 1997.

Miroff, Bruce. *Icons of Democracy: American Leaders as Heroes, Aristocrats, Dissenters, and Democrats.* Lawrence: University Press of Kansas, 2000.

Morgan, Robin. "Introduction," in *Sisterhood Is Forever: The Women's Anthology for a New Millennium,* ed. Robin Morgan. New York: Washington Square Press, 2003.

———, ed. *Sisterhood Is Forever: The Women's Anthology for a New Millennium.* New York: Washington Square Press, 2003.

Ms. Magazine. "HerStory." *Ms. Magazine.* http://www.msmagazine.com/about.asp.

National Association of Women Judges. "Statistics: 2009 Representation of United States State Court Women Judges." National Association of Women Judges. http://www.nawj.org/us_state_court_statistics_2009.asp.

National Organization for Women. "National Organization for Women PAC Endorses Obama-Biden." National Organization for Women, September 16, 2008. http://www.now.org/press/09-08/09-16.html.

———. "NOW Officers, Kim Gandy—President." National Organization for Women. http://www.now.org/officers/kg.html.

———. "NOW/PAC Endorses Carol Moseley Braun for President,

Statement of NOW/PAC Chair Kim Gandy." National Organization for Women, August 26, 2003. http://www.now.org/press/08-03/08-26.html.

National Women's Hall of Fame. "Geraldine Ferraro: Women of the Hall." National Women's Hall of Fame. http://www.greatwomen .org/women.php?action=viewone&id=61.

Neustadt, Richard. *Presidential Power and the Modern Presidents: The Politics of Leadership from Roosevelt to Reagan.* New York: Free Press, 1990.

Nichols, John. "From Muckraker to Mayor." *The Nation*, February 18, 2002. http://www.thenation.com/blogs/thebeat/18.

Norris, Pippa. "The Gender Gap: Old Challenges, New Approaches," in *Women and American Politics: New Questions, New Directions*, ed. Susan J. Carroll. New York: Oxford University Press, 2003.

———, ed. *Women, Media, and Politics.* New York: Oxford University Press, 1997.

Northouse, Peter G. *Leadership: Theory and Practice*, 4th ed. Thousand Oaks, CA: Sage, 2006.

"NOW's Woman Problem." *New York Times*, September 14, 2003.

O'Brien, David M. *Constitutional Law and Politics, Volume Two: Civil Rights and Civil Liberties*, 7th ed. New York: W. W. Norton, 2008.

———. *Storm Center: The Supreme Court in American Politics*, 8th ed. New York: W. W. Norton, 2008.

O'Connor, Anne Marie. "Hughes Answers the Call; Advisor Who Resigned to Spend More Time with Her Family Is Rejoining the Bush Team." *Los Angeles Times*, April 12, 2004, E1.

O'Connor, Karen, ed. *Women and Congress: Running, Winning, and Ruling.* New York: Haworth Press, 2001.

O'Connor, Sandra Day. *The Majesty of the Law: Reflections of a Supreme Court Justice.* New York: Random House, 2003.

Ondercin, Heather L., and Susan Welch. "Women Candidates for Congress," in "The Bottleneck: Women Becoming Candidates," in *Women and Elective Office: Past, Present, and Future*, eds. Sue Thomas and Clyde Wilcox. New York: Oxford University Press, 1998, 60–80.

Oyez. "Biography of Sandra Day O'Connor." Oyez. http://www .oyez.org/oyez/resource/legal_entity/102/biography.

Pacelle, Richard L., Jr. "A President's Legacy: Gender and Appointment to the Federal Courts," in *The Other Elites: Women, Politics, and Power in the Executive Branch*, eds. MaryAnne Borrelli and Janet M. Martin. Boulder, CO: Lynne Rienner, 1997, 147–166.

Paletz, David L. *The Media in American Politics: Contents and Consequences*, 2nd ed. New York: Longman, 2002.

Palmer, Barbara. "Justice Ruth Bader Ginsburg and the Supreme Court's Reaction to Its Second Female Member." *Women and Politics* 24, no. 1 (2002): 1–23.

———. "Women in the American Judiciary: Their Influence and Impact." *Women and Politics* 23, no. 3 (2001).

Patterson, Thomas E. "Doing Well and Doing Good: How Soft News and Critical Journalism Are Shrinking the News Audience and Weakening Democracy—And What News Outlets Can Do About It." Joan Shorenstein Center for Press, Politics, and Public Policy, John F. Kennedy School of Government, Harvard University, 2000.

———. *Out of Order.* New York: Vintage Books, 1994.

Perlez, Jane. "'Gerry, Gerry,' the Convention Chants." *New York Times,* July 20, 1984, A1.

Polsby, Nelson W., and Aaron Wildavsky. *Presidential Elections: Strategies and Structures of American Politics,* 10th ed. New York: Chatham House, 2000.

Powell, Stewart M. "Poll Finds Readiness for Female President." *Houston Chronicle,* February 20, 2006, A1.

Raasch, Chuck. "Candidates Face Distinct Challenges in Courting Female Voters." *USA Today,* September 24, 2004. http://www.usatoday.com/news/politicselections/nation/president/2004-09-24-female-voters_x.htm.

Rachanow, Shelly. *If Women Ran the World, Sh*t Would Get Done: Celebrating All the Wonderful, Amazing, Stupendous, Inspiring, Butt-kicking Things Women Do.* Newburyport, MA: Conari Press, 2006.

———. *What Would You Do If You Ran the World? Everyday Ideas from Women Who Want to Make the World a Better Place.* Newburyport, MA: Conari Press, 2009.

Reingold, Beth. *Representing Women: Sex, Gender, and Legislative Behavior in Arizona and California.* Chapel Hill: North Carolina University Press, 2000.

Rhode, Deborah L., ed. *The Difference "Difference" Makes: Women and Leadership.* Stanford, CA: Stanford University Press, 2003.

———. "Introduction," in *The Difference "Difference" Makes: Women and Leadership,* ed. Deborah L. Rhode. Stanford, CA: Stanford University Press, 2003.

———. "The Unfinished Agenda: Women and the Legal Profession." Chicago, IL: ABA Commission on Women in the Profession, 2001.

Rhode, Deborah L., and Barbara Kellerman. "Women and Leadership: The State of Play," in *Women and Leadership: The State of Play and Strategies for Change,* eds. Barbara Kellerman and Deborah L. Rhode. New York: Wiley, 2007.

Rice, Patricia. "Women Out of the Myths and into Focus," in *Women and the News,* ed. Laurily Keir Epstein. New York: Hastings House, 1978.

Rodriguez, Emelyn. "A Modern-Day Helen of Troy?" *California Journal,* June 1, 2001. http://www.statenet.com/capital-journal.

Rose Bird ProCon. "The Death Penalty." http://www.rosebirdprocon.org/.

Rosen, Ruth. *The World Split Open: How the Modern Women's Movement Changed America.* New York: Penguin Books, 2000.

Rosenbloom, Stephanie. "Evolution of a Feminist Daughter." *New York Times,* March 18, 2007. http://www.nytimes.com/2007/03/18/fashion/18walker.html?pagewanted=1&_r=3.

Rosenthal, Cindy Simon. "Getting Things Done: Women Committee Chairpersons in State Legislatures," in *Women and Elective Office: Past, Present, and Future*, eds. Sue Thomas and Clyde Wilcox. New York: Oxford University Press, 1998.

———. *When Women Lead: Integrative Leadership in State Legislatures.* New York: Oxford University Press, 1998.

———. "Women Leading Legislatures: Getting There and Getting Things Done," in *Women and Elective Office: Past, Present, and Future*, eds. Sue Thomas and Clyde Wilcox. New York: Oxford University Press, 1998, 197–212.

———, ed. *Women Transforming Congress.* Norman: University of Oklahoma Press, 2002.

Sabato, Larry J. *Feeding Frenzy: Attack Journalism and American Politics.* Baltimore, MD: Lanahan Publishers, 2000.

Sanbonmatsu, Kira. "Candidate Recruitment and Women's Election to the State Legislatures." Report prepared for the Center for American Women and Politics, Eagleton Institute of Politics, Rutgers, The State University of New Jersey, September 2003.

———. *Democrats/Republicans and the Politics of Women's Place.* Ann Arbor: University of Michigan Press, 2002.

Sapiro, Virginia. *Women in American Society: An Introduction to Women's Studies*, 5th ed. Boston: McGraw-Hill, 2003.

Schreiber, Ronnee. *Righting Feminism: Conservative Women and American Politics.* New York: Oxford University Press, 2008.

Schroeder, Pat. "Running for Our Lives: Electoral Politics," in *Sisterhood Is Forever: The Women's Anthology for a New Millennium*, ed. Robin Morgan. New York: Washington Square Press, 2003, 28–31.

Seelye, Katherine Q., and Julie Bosman. "Media Charged with Sexism in Clinton Coverage." *New York Times*, June 13, 2008, 1.

Sellers, Patricia. "Most Powerful Women in Business: Power—Do Women Really Want It?" *Fortune*, September 29, 2003. http://www.money.cnn.com/magazines/fortune/fortune_archive/200 3/10/13/350932/index.htm.

Seltzer, Richard A., Jody Newman, and Melissa Voorhees Leighton. *Sex as a Political Variable: Women as Candidates and Voters in U.S. Elections.* Boulder, CO: Lynne Rienner Publishers, 1997.

Siegal, Deborah. "Bias, Punditry, and the Press: Where Do We Go from Here?" Report from The White House Project, The Women's Media Center, and The Maynard Institute for Journalism Education, 2008. http://www.womensmediacenter.com/wmc_publications .html.

Silverstein, Mark. *Judicious Choices: The Politics of Supreme Court Confirmations*, 2nd ed. New York: W. W. Norton, 2007.

Smith, Dan. "Voters Think U.S. Ready for Woman as President." *Sacramento Bee*, March 10, 2006, A5.

Stapleton, Jean. "Introduction," in *The American Women 2001–2002: Getting to the Top*, eds. Cynthia B. Costello and Anne J. Stone. New York: W. W. Norton, 2001.

Stolberg, Sheryl Gay. "A Nation at War: The House Minority Leader; With Democrats Divided on War, Pelosi Faces Leadership Test." *New York Times*, March 31, 2003, B13.

Suellentrop, Chris. "The Leader the House Democrats Deserve," *Slate*, November 13, 2002. http://www.slate.com/id/2073934.

Sweet, Lynn. "Courting the Ladies." *Chicago Sun-Times*, October 13, 2004, 72.

———. "Did the Women's Vote Count?" *Chicago Sun-Times*, November 10, 2004, 60.

Swers, Michele L., and Carin Larson. "Women in Congress: Do They Act as Advocates for Women's Issues?" in *Women and Elective Office: Past, Present, and Future*, eds. Sue Thomas and Clyde Wilcox. New York: Oxford University Press, 1998.

Tannen, Deborah. *You Just Don't Understand: Women and Men in Conversation*. New York: Ballantine, 1990.

Tenpas, Kathryn Dunn. "Women on the White House Staff: A Longitudinal Analysis, 1939–1994," in *The Other Elites: Women, Politics, and Power in the Executive Branch*, eds. MaryAnne Borrelli and Janet M. Martin. Boulder, CO: Lynne Rienner, 1997, 91–106.

Thomas, Sue. *How Women Legislate*. New York: Oxford University Press, 1994.

———. "The Impact of Women in Political Leadership Positions," in *Women and American Politics: New Questions, New Directions*, ed. Susan J. Carroll. New York: Oxford University Press, 2003.

———. "Introduction," in *Women and Elective Office: Past, Present, and Future*, eds. Sue Thomas and Clyde Wilcox. New York: Oxford University Press, 1998.

Thomas, Sue, and Susan Welch. "The Impact of Women in State Legislatures: Numerical and Organizational Strength," in *The Impact of Women in Public Office*, ed. Susan J. Carroll. Bloomington: Indiana University Press, 2001.

Thomas, Sue, and Clyde Wilcox, eds. *Women and Elective Office: Past, Present, and Future*. New York: Oxford University Press, 1998.

———. *Women and Elective Office: Past, Present, and Future*, 2nd ed. New York: Oxford University Press, 2005.

Tindall, George Brown, and David E. Shi. *America: A Narrative History*, 4th ed. New York: W. W. Norton, 1996.

Tischler, Linda. "Where Are the Women?" *Fast Company*, February 2004, 52.

Tolleson-Rinehart, Sue. "Do Women Leaders Make a Difference?" in *The Impact of Women in Public Office*, ed. Susan J. Carroll. Bloomington: Indiana University Press, 2001, 149–165.

Tong, Rosemarie Putnam. *Feminist Thought: A More Comprehensive Introduction*, 2nd ed. Boulder, CO: Westview, 1998.

Tuchman, Gaye. *Hearth and Home: Images of Women in the News Media*. New York: Oxford University Press, 1978.

US House of Representatives. "Biography of Congresswoman Loretta Sanchez." US House of Representatives. http://www.lorettasanchez

.house.gov/index.php?option=com_content&view=article&id=18& Itemid=53.

Walker, Rebecca. "The Power of Palin." Huffington Post, September 22, 2008. http://www.huffingtonpost.com/rebecca-walker/the-power-of -palin_b_128377.html.

———, ed. *To Be Real: Telling the Truth and Changing the Face of Feminism.* New York: Anchor Books, 1995.

Waterman, Richard W., Robert Wright, and Gilbert St. Clair. *The Image-Is-Everything Presidency: Dilemmas in American Leadership.* Boulder, CO: Westview Press, 1999.

Watson, Robert P. *The Presidents' Wives: Reassessing the Office of First Lady.* Boulder, CO: Lynne Rienner Publishers, 2000.

Watson, Robert P., and Ann Gordon, eds. *Anticipating Madam President.* Boulder, CO: Lynne Rienner Publishers, 2003.

Wayne, Stephen J. *The Road to the White House 2008: The Politics of Presidential Elections.* Belmont, CA: Thomson Wadsworth, 2008.

Weaver, David. "Women as Journalists," in *Women, Media, and Politics,* ed. Pippa Norris. New York: Oxford University Press, 1997.

Weinraub, Bernard. "Mississippi Farm Topic: Does She Bake Muffins?" *New York Times,* August 2, 1984, 16.

Whicker, Marcia Lynn, and Malcolm Jewell. "The Feminization of Leadership in State Legislatures," in *Women and Elective Office: Past, Present, and Future,* eds. Sue Thomas and Clyde Wilcox. New York: Oxford University Press, 1998.

Whitaker, Lois Duke. "Women and Sex Stereotypes: Cultural Reflections in the Mass Media," in *Women in Politics: Outsiders or Insiders?* 4th ed., ed. Lois Duke Whitaker. Upper Saddle River, NJ: Prentice Hall, 2006.

———, ed. *Women in Politics: Outsiders or Insiders?* 4th ed. Upper Saddle River, NJ: Prentice Hall, 2006.

Whitney, Catherine, et. al. *Nine and Counting: The Women of the Senate.* New York: William Morrow, 2000.

Wier, Sara J. "Women Governors in the 21st Century: Re-Examining the Pathways to the Presidency," in *Women in Politics: Outsiders or Insiders?* 4th ed., ed. Lois Duke Whitaker. Upper Saddle River, NJ: Prentice Hall, 2006, 226–237.

Wilson, Marie C. *Closing the Leadership Gap: Why Women Can and Must Help Run the World.* New York: Penguin, 2004.

Winfield, Betty Houchin. "The First Lady, Political Power, and the Media: Who Elected Her Anyway?" in *Women, Media, and Politics,* ed. Pippa Norris. New York: Oxford University Press, 1997, 166–179.

Wolffe, Richard. *Renegade: The Making of a President.* New York: Crown Publishers, 2009.

Women's Voices. Women Vote. "Unmarried Women Play Critical Role in Historic Election," Women's Voices. Women Vote. http://www.wvwv.org/research-items/unmarried-women-change-america.

Index

About the Book

Nancy Pelosi's rise to speaker of the House of Representatives, Hillary Clinton's presidential campaign: clearly women are moving to center stage in US politics. In this wide-ranging text, Lori Cox Han explores whether—and if so, how—their presence is changing the political process.

Han first provides a solid context, thoroughly covering the history of the women's movement, suffrage, the contours of feminism, and issues of equality. She then turns to women as voters, activists, candidates, officeholders, and policymakers and provides a broad yet gendered look at both mass politics and political institutions.

Substantially expanded and updated, this new edition

- offers thorough grounding in political science scholarship
- considers women in all arenas of government
- addresses diversity—including ideological diversity—in the women's movement
- includes biographical profiles of prominent women leaders

Throughout, Han highlights women's political leadership to engage students and stimulate classroom discussion about women's role in the operation of our governing institutions.

Lori Cox Han is professor of political science at Chapman University. Her publications include *Rethinking Madam President* (coedited with Caroline Heldman) and *Governing from Center Stage*.